TEACHING SOMEONE TO DRIVE

How To Books for Family Reference

Arranging Insurance
Becoming a Father
Buying a Personal Computer
Cash from Your Computer
Choosing a Nursing Home
Choosing a Package Holiday
Dealing with a Death in the Family
How to Apply to an Industrial
   Tribunal
How to be a Local Councillor
How to be an Effective School
   Governor
How to Claim State Benefits
How to Lose Weight & Keep Fit
How to Plan a Wedding

How to Raise Funds & Sponsorship
How to Run a Local Campaign
How to Run a Voluntary Group
How to Survive Divorce
How to Take Care of Your Heart
How to Use the Internet
Making a Complaint
Making a Video
Making a Wedding Speech
Managing Your Personal Finances
Successful Grandparenting
Successful Single Parenting
Taking In Students
Teaching Someone to Drive
Winning Consumer Competitions

Other titles in preparation

The How To series now contains more than 200 titles in the following categories:

Business Basics
Family Reference
Jobs & Careers
Living & Working Abroad
Student Handbooks
Successful Writing

Please send for a free copy of the latest catalogue for full details (see back cover for address).

FAMILY REFERENCE

TEACHING SOMEONE TO DRIVE

How to prepare a learner driver safely
and successfully for the driving test

Angela Oatridge

How To Books

Cartoons by Mike Flanagan

British Library Cataloguing in Publication Data
A catalogue record for this book is available from the British Library.

© Copyright 1997 by Angela Oatridge.

First published in 1997 by How To Books Ltd, Plymbridge House,
Estover Road, Plymouth PL6 7PZ, United Kingdom.
Tel: (01752) 202301. Fax: (01752) 202331.

Note: The material contained in this book is set out in good faith for
general guidance and no liability can be accepted for loss or expense
incurred as a result of relying in particular circumstances on statements
made in the book. The laws and regulations are complex and liable to
change, and readers should check the current position with the relevant
authorities before making personal arrangements.

Produced for How To Books by Deer Park Productions.
Typeset by PDQ Typesetting, Stoke-on-Trent, Staffs.
Printed and bound by Cromwell Press, Broughton Gifford, Melksham,
Wiltshire.

Contents

List of Illustrations

Preface

Driving and learning to drive, like reading and learning to read, is one of the biggest steps towards a fuller life; like reading, driving is one of those skills which once mastered seem very easy. Few people remember struggling with early reading books and most drivers end up driving so automatically that they can hardly remember how they were initially taught to drive.

This book is a step by step guide on how to teach someone to drive, from the first introduction to the car to the skills of parking and motorway driving. Each page is another step on the ladder to turning a novice driver into becoming a safe and courteous driver, and to enabling both you and your learner to enjoy what should be an interesting and rewarding experience.

Always remember when accompanying a learner driver to be patient, tolerant and understanding at all times. Shouting, sarcasm, verbal and physical abuse is not teaching: such bullying tactics will not only mean that the student takes longer to learn but could put them off learning at all or even result in an accident.

Angela M Oatridge BA, ADI, MIAM

Is This You?

Friend

Relative

Partner

Neighbour

Instructor

Car owner

Full licence holder

Insured to drive

Responsible

Patient

Trustworthy

Vigilant

Good eyesight

Good hearing

Tolerant

Calm in a crisis

Quick reflexes

Self disciplined

Practical

Courteous

Alert

Mature

Good helper

1
Getting Started

ADOPTING THE RIGHT ATTITUDE

Driving and learning to drive is, along with reading and learning to read, one of the biggest steps to a fuller and more interesting life. However, like reading, driving is one of those skills which once mastered seem very easy. Few people can remember struggling with Janet and John or other early reading books, and very few drivers can remember all the little details of how they were taught driving.

This book is a step by step guide to help your learner become a safe and courteous driver.

Presenting yourself correctly

Before sitting beside a learner driver it is important to create an atmosphere of confidence and stability for the learner. A person learning to drive is usually very nervous, although often they will try to hide their nervousness by chatting, or even appearing over confident. If you are nervous about accompanying a learner driver the learner will feel it, and it will affect their driving.

A clean tidy appearance will help gain the respect and confidence of your learner. You are in close contact with people in a confined space for fairly long periods so remember:

- smoking
- bad breath
- body odours

can distress your learner and interfere with their concentration, which in turn will delay progress.

Having the right attitude

At all times the instructor or person sitting with a learner driver must apply:

- patience
- tolerance
- understanding of the student's problems.

Shouting and physical abuse is not teaching: bullying of any description could cause a student to take much longer to learn, and often results in accidents.

Explaining why

Always recap on what you did on the previous lesson and build on it. Ensure your learner knows *why* they must do a thing, not let them just do it parrot fashion. For example, mirrors – to just keep saying 'check your mirror' without having explained why, or the advantages of knowing what is happening behind and to the side, could lead to your learner believing, subconsciously, that mirrors are of little importance. Once through the test, they may never use mirrors correctly, perhaps resulting in an accident.

If you feel your learner is not making progress, change tactics, use another method of explaining. Make sure you use a variety of routes, so that your learner has to deal with different road and traffic conditions, and learns how to 'read the road ahead'.

Each lesson should contain all the skills that your student has learned so far.

Never teach anyone just to pass the test. Teach them a skill for life, which is 'To be an observant, safe and considerate driver'.

PREPARING ROUTES

Before taking a learner driver out it is a good idea to plan a variety of routes to cover the various skills they need to learn.

Nursery routes

- A very quiet road, preferably with a long straight run, and no parked cars. An empty car park on a Sunday can be handy: however, make sure you get your learner to drive out of the car park and along the normal road before the session ends.

- Progress onto roads with a little traffic and left turns.

When you first start right turns use roads which have a marked waiting area if at all possible: it gives the learner confidence, and they can see the advantage of good positioning.

Intermediate routes

- Longer drives through various road types, quiet roads with hidden dangers, for example:- unmarked crossroads, schools in the area or an old people's home.

- Wide fairly quiet road to practise turning in the road: modern housing estates are usually ideal.

- A fairly quiet road with side roads on the left and occasional parked cars, to practise reversing and parking between cars.

- Town traffic with lights and right turns, to help with your learner's concentration, observation and anticipation.

Advanced routes

- Dual carriageways with turnings off to the left and right, so your learner appreciates the dangers of entering, crossing, leaving and driving along a dual carriageway.

- Heavy town traffic, with buses stopping and pulling out, traffic hold ups and pedestrians jay walking. This will help with forward planning, correct use of mirrors, signals and gears, as well as observation, anticipation and clutch control.

- Simulated test routes, to incorporate all the items on an actual test route; however, do not drive over the actual routes the examiners use. To use real test routes all the time is unfair to people actually taking their driving test, and also gives your learner a false sense of their capabilities.

- Finally, just before the actual driving test, a couple of practice drives along the route you think the examiner might take. However, this is not essential, as if you have taught your pupil correctly over a variety of roads and traffic conditions they should be able to drive safely and well, on any route.

> People taught only over test routes tend to lack anticipation, observation and forward planning when they drive in a strange town.

USING A SUITABLE VEHICLE

Type of car

Dual controls
Ideally we should have a dual control car to learn to drive in. However, unless you intend to teach more than one or more people, it could prove an unnecessary expense. If you explain things carefully, are patient and gently build up your learner's knowledge, you should have no problems.

Four forward gears
A car with only four forward gears is ideal; at the early stages, and when under pressure, pupils can inadvertently select fifth gear in error, resulting in a build up of tension.

Size of car
A medium or small sized car is ideal: Metros, Golfs and Polos, for example, all have superb gear changes. It's handy to have a normal floor gear stick rather than one on the steering column, as it's easier for you to see if your learner starts to select the incorrect gear.

Boots and bonnets
Cars with very long bonnets or long boots can cause problems to a learner. A long bonnet means having to creep out a long way to get maximum vision when leaving a side road, and long boots can cause problems when parking as it's difficult to see the end of the car.

Safety checks and paperwork

- Any car you are taking a learner out in should be well serviced: nothing is worse for a learner than trying to drive a car which is faulty in any way.

- Regularly check brakes, clutches and tyres.

- Ensure that you have plenty of petrol in the tank, particularly in the early stage of lessons. Later your learner can practise filling the car; however, in the initial stages, this could cause problems and stress to a learner driver.

- Always clean all windows and lights before taking a learner out. Maximum vision is vitally important.

• Make sure the car is insured for a learner driver.

• Make sure your learner's provisional licence is signed.

Extra accessories
In an ideal world all learner drivers would learn in a dual controlled car; however, this is not always practical or possible. Items which are not expensive but essential when teaching or helping someone learn to drive are:

• an extra interior mirror on the passenger's side: this is essential as it gives the instructor a full picture of what is happening behind (stick on mirrors can be obtained from most car accessory outlets)

• a notebook and pencil so you can sketch information for your learner, *eg* correct positioning before turning right or reduced field of vision when driving too close to another vehicle.

• an up-to-date copy of *The Highway Code*, the driver's bible

• the booklet called *The Driving Test* produced by the DSA (Driving Standards Agency)

• *The Driving Manual* also produced by the DSA.

TAKING PREVENTATIVE MEASURES

If lessons are planned carefully, and plenty of notice is given in the early stages of any left or right turn, or even advice as to the suitability of a certain gear, then you will find that the time spent with your learner will be without too many problems, even enjoyable. However, a few basic rules can help both you and the learner.

Your tone of voice
A student normally needs to be told to correct an error in a quiet but firm voice; shouting or any hint of anger in your voice will often make the student worry, even panic, worsening the situation and causing more problems to both instructor and learner.

Understanding your learner's anxieties
People are very sensitive when learning to drive: they are adults trying to learn a skill which the majority of their peers seem to have

achieved with ease. Learning to drive is a lonely experience, most learners feel they are the only ones who make so many errors.

Teaching by example
A learner will often lose heart, even give up learning, if repeatedly making the same error. If you find this is happening to your learner, for example, oversteering on left turns, try an entirely different approach. Let the learner watch you do a couple of tight left turns, and explain exactly what you are doing and why.

Dealing with panic
If your pupil panics suddenly, stop the car at the side of the road, calm things down, then explain carefully exactly what went wrong. Keep a packet of mints handy: it's very reassuring to the student when you can say, 'let's enjoy a mint, and talk about what happened'.

Intervening
There are two forms of intervention:

- physical, when you actually do something to control the situation, *ie* have to take hold of the steering wheel or use the brakes,

- non physical, when you tell the student what to do.

Physical intervention
If you are using a car fitted with dual control pedals:

- always explain why you needed to use the dual control
- always check your mirror before you use the dual control
- remember dual controls are for emergency, or to help in demonstration; never use them instead of explaining to a student – you are there to instruct, not to drive
- an example of when you may need a dual control is when your student is approaching a hazard too fast and fails to slow down on request.

Other forms of physical intervention
To correct steering
  – be careful not to touch your student when correcting steering
  – to correct to right, place your hand low on wheel and push
  – to correct to left place your hand high on wheel and pull.

To brake
- if you feel you need to use the hand brake to slow your pupil down, remember that the hand brake only operates on the rear wheels, so the car could pull to the side: it's far better to try to control the situation by verbal instruction.

To help with gear change
- when wrong gear is selected at a critical time
- when your student is experiencing difficulty in selecting gear.

In both the above cases check that your student has the clutch pressed down.

To indicate
- operating the indicator to prevent a dangerous situation, *eg* wrong indicator selected, or indicator not cancelled.

To help with the hand brake
- sometimes a nervous student may have difficulty putting the hand brake on fully or taking it off: remember you often just need to lift it a little to press in the button.

Non-physical intervention
The spoken word is the most valuable tool you have: the way you use it, and the degree of firmness, can convey much to your student.

- Gears
  - if your student has not selected a gear suitable to the situation, a gentle but firm 'third gear' or whatever gear is necessary will be enough
  - never leave it too late to correct gear selection: a learner will take longer than an experienced drive to select the right gear
  - never change gear while turning.

Always impress on students the importance of being in the right gear at the right time.

- windscreen wipers
  - students so often forget they have wipers, always remind them if it starts to rain

- lights
  - remind students about putting on dipped headlights in rain, fog or poor light

- Mirrors
    - you can never emphasise enough the importance of mirrors.

CHECKLIST

Have you:
- a suitable car
- made sure your student has a current provisional licence
- checked your student can read a number plate from over 20 metres
- fitted an extra inside mirror for the use of instruction
- the appropriate paper, pencil and books in the car?

QUESTIONS AND ANSWERS

Q *My car is a 1970 Vauxhall Viva – will I be able to use it to teach my daughter?*

A Providing the car is in good mechanical order this will be a very good car to teach in. The Vivas were very popular for driving schools as they had a very positive gear change. However, do check the hand brake regularly, as you may find that your student has difficulty pulling it fully on or releasing it on a hill.

Q *My wife would love to drive; however, because of an accident in her childhood, she has difficulty moving her left foot. Is it possible for her to have a car specially fitted for her disability?*

A Most disabilities should not prevent a person from learning to drive and your nearest Disabled Drivers' Assessment Centre will give specialist advice. In your case you may find that an automatic car will be perfect for your wife, as she will only need to use one foot to drive.

Q *I have been living in Australia for the last 15 years, and have an Australian driving licence. Do I have to take the driving test again to drive in the UK?*

A A driving licence issued in Australia may be exchanged for an ordinary British driving licence within one year of taking up United Kingdom residence. This concession applies to all EU residents and those of certain other countries including New Zealand, Hong Kong and Malta. A full list of countries can be obtained from the licensing authority.

CASE STUDIES

Throughout this book we will be using fictional case studies to show how three imaginary people with very different backgrounds and ideas are helping to teach someone to drive.

Julie Sutherland

Julie Sutherland, 35, is a community nurse and has held a full driving licence for ten years. She has been asked by friends, neither of whom drive, if she would take their 18-year-old daughter, Susan Gray, out for some driving lessons. Susan, a trainee nurse, is a very shy, quiet girl.

Philip Napier

Philip Napier, 42, wants to teach his wife Tessa to drive, also his 17-year-old son Mark. Philip has been made redundant from his firm and intends to use the redundancy money to start a taxi business. He will therefore need the help of his wife, and later his sons, in the business. His wife is a very confident woman, but is a little apprehensive about learning to drive, as in her late teens she and a friend who was teaching her were involved in a serious accident, resulting in her being in hospital for many months.

Thomas McPherson

Thomas McPherson, a 26-year-old student, is helping his 22-year-old brother Martin to get through his driving test. Thomas passed his test first time at 18 after a course of lessons with a local driving school. Martin also had a course of lessons when he was 18, but failed his test, and soon after went to Gibraltar with the Royal Air Force. Martin is now out of the RAF and needs to pass his test to obtain a good job.

DISCUSSION POINTS

1. List five ways you could prepare yourself before accompanying a learner driver.

2. Do you feel that teaching someone to drive will improve your own driving?

3. How important do you feel it is to be relaxed when teaching driving?

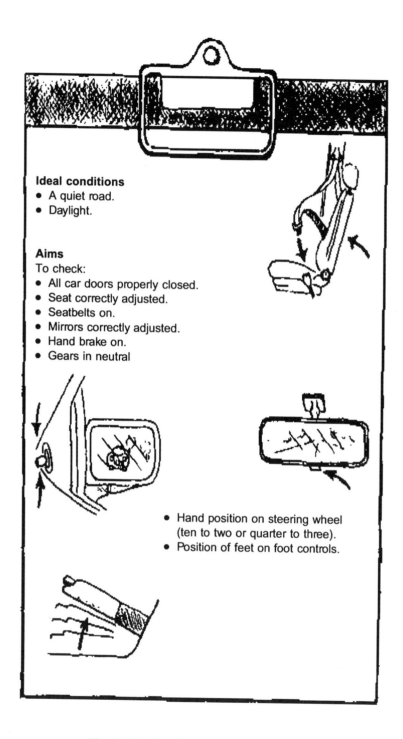

Ideal conditions
- A quiet road.
- Daylight.

Aims

To check:
- All car doors properly closed.
- Seat correctly adjusted.
- Seatbelts on.
- Mirrors correctly adjusted.
- Hand brake on.
- Gears in neutral

- Hand position on steering wheel (ten to two or quarter to three).
- Position of feet on foot controls.

Fig. 1. Adopting the correct driving position.

2
Introducing the Car

GETTING TO KNOW THE CONTROLS

Ideally this should take place in a quiet road during daylight hours. Your aims should be:

- to relax your pupil

- to explain where all the controls are

- to help the student understand the importance of all the controls including:

  dashboard instruments
  indicators
  four way flashers
  horn
  washers and wipers
  lights
  mirrors
  foot controls
  hand brake
  gear lever.

Helping pupils to relax

All pupils, regardless of how much driving they have done, should be reintroduced to a car which they have not driven before. The amount of time spent on this will largely depend on the knowledge each person has about cars and driving generally.

Ask the pupil to sit in the driving seat while you explain the controls: they are then able to look directly at everything you are talking about. Remove the ignition key at this stage as a nervous learner might inadvertently turn the ignition on.

Explaining the hand controls

Looking at the fascia panel
It is best to start with the dials on the fascia panel as this relaxes the pupil. Tell them that you do not expect them to remember everything at this stage, and that you will write a little reminder at the end of the lesson.

Explain about the warning lights on the panel and emphasise their importance, which is to tell the driver something. Examples you could give are:

1. The oil pressure warning light comes on to warn you that oil pressure is lost, and to continue driving could cause expensive damage to the engine, therefore the amount of oil in the engine must be checked immediately.

2. The battery warning light lights up if the alternator is no longer producing the electricity which provides power to the battery. This could cause the battery to run flat (lose its power) in a very short time, resulting in no lights which could eventually contribute to an extremely dangerous situation.

Remind your student that when the ignition is turned on all the warning lights will glow to show everything is in working order; once the engine is running they should go out.

The steering wheel
The way we hold the steering wheel is very important. If the hands are held too low, or only one hand is on the wheel, then in the event of a skid, tyre blow out or being hit by another car, control will be lost immediately and the car will most likely spin out of control, and may even turn over.

The ideal position for the hands, using the clock face for an example, is ten to two or quarter to three (see Figure 2).

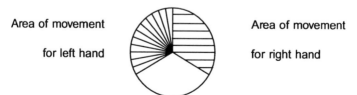

Fig. 2. The correct way to hold the steering wheel.

Explain that when turning the wheel a push and pull method must be used, the right hand not going above the twelve o'clock position or below the twenty-past-the-hour point, the left hand not going beyond twelve or below the twenty-to-the-hour position.

Explain why we often use headlights (dipped) during the day when it is raining, dull or foggy. Point out that this does not help drivers to see better: it helps other road users, including pedestrians, to see cars more easily.

The gears
When showing position of the gears explain the ideal way to hold the hand over the gear lever. This will help in selecting the correct gear and avoid all the problems learner drivers have when they accidentally select the wrong gear:

- when selecting first or second gear the driver should keep the hand cupped to the right, to push the gear lever to the left

- when selecting third or fourth gear the driver should cup the hand to the left of the gear lever, so it is being pulled towards them.

It's a good idea to draw the gear positions on a piece of paper and prop it on the dashboard, so that your learner does not have to take their eyes off the road to look down at the gears.

Explaining the foot controls
Use the A B C method to show the position of the feet: the right foot is used for A (accelerator) and B (foot brake); the left foot is used exclusively for C (the clutch).

Point out that you cannot stop and go at the same time, thus it is logical to use the right foot for both the accelerator, which makes you move, and the foot brake, which is used to slow down or stop the car.

Using examples
Always give plenty of ideas to demonstrate exactly what you mean, for example you can explain that if the learner feels that the car is running away, then as a horserider would pull on the reins of a horse which was getting out of hand, a driver gently brakes until the correct speed is achieved, holding firmly on the 'reins' (steering wheel) at all times.

A lot of learners worry that the car will stop if they take their foot off the **accelerator**, or will stall if they use the foot brake. An ideal example to use would be the bicycle: when riding a bicycle if you feel you are going too fast, you stop pedalling (stop accelerating) and apply the brakes gently. When you are satisfied with your speed you start to pedal (accelerate) again. The same applies with the car: you can slow down gently, using the foot brake, then accelerate (pedal) again when you are at the correct speed for the situation.

The bicycle can also be used as an example of the importance of applying the **foot brake** with a gentle action. Every cyclist knows that if you pull on the brakes too harshly, you will fly over the handlebars. When driving a car if you apply the brakes hard, everything that is loose in the car ends up on the floor, the passengers become upset, and you stand a greater risk of being hit in the rear by the car behind.

The left foot is used exclusively for the **clutch** which you could compare to a gate. You need to open the gate (push in the clutch) each time you change gear, remembering not to slam it (snatch your foot off it) when you close it.

Explaining the foot and hand brakes
Explain that the foot brake and hand brake are entirely different: the foot brake is used for slowing down or stopping; the hand brake is only used when you are stationary, as a parking brake.

Point out that when you stop you need to keep two hands on the wheel to keep the car under control. The foot brake works on all four wheels, the hand brake only affects the rear wheels, and to try to stop on the hand brake could not only cause the car to veer to the side, but would also mean that the driver has only one hand on the wheel, so the car could spin out of control.

TAKING BASIC PRECAUTIONS BEFORE STARTING THE ENGINE

Learning about the basic checks necessary before starting the engine, and understanding why we do them, are essential for the safety of the learner driver and other road users. As a pilot of an aeroplane has a list of cockpit checks he must make before taking off, we as drivers also have checks which we must always make when we get into the driving seat of a car. A pilot has to have a long list; however drivers have such a short list that after a while they become automatic.

Making the five basic checks
The five major checks are:

- all doors are closed properly
- seat is correctly adjusted and seat belts on
- mirrors are correctly adjusted
- hand brake is on
- gear lever is in neutral.

Always give a logical reason for anything you ask your learner to do, such as the following:

Doors
It is so easy to half shut a door: often people in a hurry, or while unloading a car, just tap the door shut. If while you were driving a door flew open, not only could it cause a serious accident by perhaps knocking a cyclist off his bike, but it could distract the driver. Therefore one must always quickly check all doors are properly closed.

Seat
If the seat is not correctly adjusted, the driver may find that they keep stalling or over accelerating the car. Legs and arms may start to ache, plus the concentration required to drive safely will be impeded.

Seat belts
It is the law not only in the United Kingdom but in many other parts of the world that seat belts should be worn. The wearing of seat belts not only saves lives, but it helps deportment by stopping you slumping in your seat. You could also point out that the driver should remind passengers to put on their seat belts.

Mirrors
The mirror gives eyes in the back of your head. It is very important to know not only what is happening or going to happen in front of you, but also what is happening behind and either side of the car. It would also be a good idea for your student to see how side mirrors, which are mainly convex mirrors, not only give a wider view, but make the vehicles behind look smaller, so they could be a lot closer than you think. The interior mirror is flat glass so gives a truer picture.

Hand brake
The hand brake must always be firmly on; if it is only partly on, and you are on a slope, as you put the gears into neutral before starting

the engine you could roll backward or forwards, rolling into another car or even a pedestrian.

Gear in neutral
If the gear lever is not in neutral when you start the engine, the car will jump forward, or backwards, depending which gear you are in. It is therefore very important to check your gear position before starting the engine.

- If you stall the car always apply the hand brake and put the gear in neutral before trying to start the engine again.

These checks can be in any order, except the last two: you must always check the hand brake is firmly on before checking the gear.

MOVING STRAIGHT AHEAD FROM STATIONARY

Moving forward under control, and stopping smoothly, are perhaps the most important stages of learning to drive, therefore be prepared to spend time and patience on these fundamental parts of driving when you are with a rank beginner.

The ideal place to start off for a new driver is a quiet level road. The learner's aims are to:

- show awareness of traffic hazards by the correct use of mirrors, signals and shoulder checks
- engage first gear smoothly and quietly
- operate clutch gently
- move off smoothly without jerking, wheel spin, or stalling
- avoid over-revving of engine.

Moving forward on a level road: the basics
1. Do the cockpit checks.

2. Start the engine then ask the learner to gently place the right foot on A (accelerator) to obtain the correct 'purr' of the engine. You could mention that over acceleration will produce a lion's roar which not only sounds frightening to a learner, but makes them sound bad tempered (like shouting). Over acceleration is also bad for the engine.

3. Your student should now push the clutch right in with the left foot, hold it there and put the gear lever into first gear position.

Hands should return immediately to the steering wheel after any gear change. If your student stalls the car always remind him to apply the hand brake and put the gear lever back to the neutral position before re-starting the engine.

4. Make sure the student checks mirrors and shoulder before releasing the hand brake.

5. A smooth pull away is obtained by the gentle movement of the clutch pedal. It is important at this initial stage that your learner lifts the clutch foot up very slowly, even as the car starts to move. A fast movement on the clutch could result in a kangaroo hop or a stall. Your student should understand that the clutch and accelerator pedals operate in a see-saw manner: when lifting the clutch foot up a little pressure is required on the accelerator by pushing it down a fraction.

   Make sure both your learner's hands are on the wheel before the clutch is fully lifted to ensure a smooth pull away, under control.

6. Releasing the hand brake is always the last thing your learner should do before moving off; applying it is the first thing to do when they have stopped.

STOPPING UNDER CONTROL

The learner's aims will be to:

- stop the vehicle smoothly
  - under control
  - without riding the clutch
  - without coasting
  - without stalling
- give the correct signal as laid down in the *Highway Code*
- use the hand and foot controls correctly
- stop in a suitable position on the road
- use the mirror correctly.

Stopping under control: the basics

1. Decide in advance a suitable place to stop (refer to the *Highway Code* if in doubt).

2. Your learner should always check the mirror to ensure that by stopping they will not cause problems to anyone behind.

3. The left indicator should be used to show intention to pull over to the left and stop.

4. The right foot should be moved from A (accelerator) to B (foot brake) and light pressure applied.

5. The clutch is then pushed in with the left foot just before the final halt on the foot brake.

6. Two hands must be kept on the wheel to control the steering until the car has completely stopped.

7. The learner must keep his/her feet firmly on the foot brake and clutch until the hand brake is applied and the gear lever is returned to neutral.

At this point explain how stop lights on cars can help keep accidents down and the importance of making sure they are in working order.

Practising starts and stops

If this is a very first lesson it is best to practise starting, driving along and stopping until the pupil feels at ease with the foot and hand movements. A little time spent at this stage can save hours of frustration later on.

A new driver will need to be talked through this a few times until finding a rhythm to the movements of feet, hands and eyes. After a couple of times, suggest the driver tells you what he/she is going to do next.

Pupils who have driven before will spend very little time on this; however, do ensure they understand the basic rules: the cockpit checks, the correct position of hands on the wheel and observation on pulling out from stop.

PREVENTING ACCIDENTS WITH DOORS

Make sure your pupil understands:

- the driver's responsibility regarding doors
- why we must warn passengers before they open a door either on entering or leaving a vehicle
- the importance of observation when passing a stationary vehicle
- why we must keep a reasonable distance away from parked vehicles.

You should explain to your pupil that:

- an open door can double the width of a car
- opening a nearside door could harm pedestrians or a cyclist passing on the near side of the car
- opening an offside door could cause an accident if opened in the path of an oncoming vehicle
- the driver is responsible for the actions of passengers entering or leaving the vehicle.

CHECKLIST

At the end of this session your pupil should understand:

- the five basic cockpit checks
- the position of feet on controls
- the position of the various gears
- how to hold the gear lever correctly when changing gear
- the correct sequence of movements to move off
- the correct sequence of movements to stop.

QUESTIONS AND ANSWERS

Q *My pupil is very small, and cannot reach the foot pedals properly. What can I do?*

A A firm cushion behind your pupil's back will help push the body forward. If this will not work, try fixing small blocks to the pedals; however, do make sure they are fixed securely.

Q *My aunt is 62 years old and wants to learn to drive. Is she too old to start learning now?*

A There is no upper age limit in learning to drive, however, older people do take longer to learn, but they are usually a delight to teach, and once taught become good drivers.

Q *I notice you recommend teaching in daylight during the early lessons – why?*

A A beginner has enough to worry about without the extra dangers of driving at night, when oncoming lights and poorer vision add to the many new things a learner has to cope with. A learner will progress more quickly if starting their lessons in daylight.

CASE STUDIES

Julie finds teaching is hard work

Julie's pupil, Susan, has never sat behind the wheel of a car before.

She is a very quiet, nervous girl. 'I found this a lot more work than I thought it would be. Susan was very nervous the whole time, although I think started to relax when I was explaining the controls. At the first attempt at moving off, she took her foot too quickly off the clutch, and stalled the car. However, after a couple more attempts, with me explaining each stage, she managed to do it perfectly, although very slowly.'

Philip narrowly avoids a domestic quarrel

Philip is taking his wife, Tessa, for driving practice. Tessa's serious car accident in her teens put her off learning to drive until now. 'Tessa was very nervous initially, and at one stage I was afraid that the whole exercise was going to end up in a domestic argument, as she said I was talking down to her, treating her like a ten year old. Once I explained that this was really the basics of driving, and it would be easier and more interesting after this initial lesson, everything went like clockwork.'

Thomas and Martin discover why Martin may have failed his test

Thomas is taking his brother Martin out for driving practice. Martin failed his driving test three years ago, but is very confident that he will pass the test he has applied for next month. 'Initially I thought the introduction to the car would be a waste of time, as Martin has done a lot of driving, even taken a test. However, it proved to be valuable. I realised straight away that Martin was not holding the steering wheel correctly – in fact when we started to move, his hands were all over the place. I think this could be one of the reason he failed his test.'

DISCUSSION POINTS

1. What are the advantages of always doing the basic cockpit checks in the same order?

2. Why do we always try to keep two hands on the wheel at all times?

3. The foot brake should always be applied firmly but gently – can you think why?

4. Why do you think it important to stop your learner looking down at the gears at this early stage?

An example of the type of sketch, and notes, which a learner could take home at the end of a first lesson. This is a reminder about what to do in preparation for the next lesson.

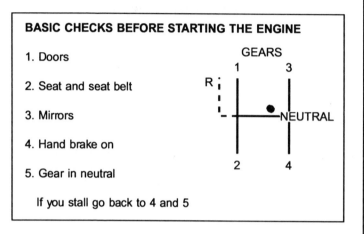

BASIC CHECKS BEFORE STARTING THE ENGINE

1. Doors

2. Seat and seat belt

3. Mirrors

4. Hand brake on

5. Gear in neutral

If you stall go back to 4 and 5

GEARS

1   3

R

NEUTRAL

2   4

- Practise at home by trying to coordinate the left and right foot in a see-saw motion while sitting down.

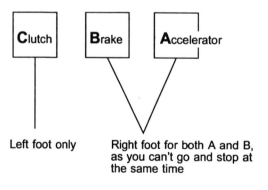

Clutch   Brake   Accelerator

Left foot only   Right foot for both A and B, as you can't go and stop at the same time

Fig. 3. Suggested homework for your student.

3
Coordinating Eyes, Feet and Hands

TEACHING GEAR-CHANGING

Once your learner has done a few starts and stops, try to get them to change into second gear as soon as the car starts moving. You may find a new driver rolls to a stop initially: however, do not worry – after a couple of attempts they will start to do it much quicker. It's a good idea to have a set order of commands.

1. Clutch in
2. Push your gear lever into second gear:
   – don't look down, keep you eyes on the road
   – hand back on steering wheel
3. Lift your clutch up.

If your learner is steering badly, advise looking much further down the road. Many learners think they should look just in front of the car. As the road bends a new driver may either under- or over-steer. As one is normally in first or second gear at this early stage this is easy to correct. If necessary help with the steering and use the command:

• Take your foot off the accelerator.

Most people get used to the amount of pull and push they need on the steering wheel.
   Your pupil's aims will be to:

• select the correct gear at the correct time
• engage gear smoothly
   – without labouring the engine
   – without jerking or noise
   – without looking down at the gear stick
• maintain a steady course while steering
• coordinate the use of clutch, accelerator and hands
• avoiding riding the clutch, coasting or over-revving the engine.

Underlining the importance of mirrors

When driving it is important always to check mirrors before any change of speed, so do explain to your learner that this is to ensure that his action in slowing down or going faster will not cause problems to any motorist behind – for example:

- the motorist behind is travelling too close – if you slow down quickly it could cause him to drive into your rear bumper

- the motorist behind has signalled his intention to overtake you; if you decide to increase speed it could cause a serious accident.

Explaining about changing gear

After a gear change the hand must be returned immediately to the steering wheel. (Two hands should be on the wheel at all times when the car is moving, except for the seconds it takes to actually change the gear.)

When changing gear it is advisable to have the palm of the hand to the right of the gear knob when using first and second gear, and to the left when using the third or fourth gear. This makes it easier to select the required gear.

On a five gear box it can be very easy to select fifth gear instead of third. If your pupil has difficulty with this, please be very patient, it can be very frustrating and upsetting to a learner.

To explain gears you could compare them to running along a busy pavement. You start with small steps (first gear), then gradually take longer and longer steps if there is nothing in the way: however, if you run around a corner you need to take smaller strides (a lower gear). If you think about it it would be impossible to run around a corning keeping the same length of step, also the tighter the corner the smaller step one would take (see Figure 4).

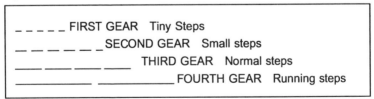

Fig. 4. Looking at gears as steps.

This easy example will help a learner driver understand why we need different gears in different circumstances.

You can stop in any gear, depending on the circumstances. If, for example you were approaching traffic lights which had just turned red, then third gear would be quite in order. However, initially it is best if a learner comes down to second gear to stop.

You can change from fourth gear directly to second, but must adjust your speed with the foot brake first.

MOVING OFF ON A HILL

Your pupil's aims will be to:

- move off smoothly on an incline or hill without rolling back, over accelerating or stalling
- to coordinate the use of clutch, hand brake and accelerator
- use the mirror, signals and shoulder checks correctly
- be aware at all times of other road users
- understand use of the clutch.

Mastering hill starts

Moving off on a slope or hill is a skill which should be practised until perfect. It is important that the pupil should be able to feel and hear 'the biting point', where the clutch plates are just touching. An ideal sequence to teach your learner is as follows:

1. With the engine running, clutch right in, engage first gear.
2. Put a little pressure on the accelerator, listen for a purring sound.
3. Check mirror, signal to pull away.
4. Lift clutch up to biting point. Listen to engine sound.
5. Hold in this position, check shoulder and mirror, release hand brake.
6. A fraction more pressure on the accelerator, then clutch up the rest of the way slowly.

Stalling

Stalling can happen at stage 4 if the clutch is lifted up too far, or at stage 6 when many pupils forget to put a little extra pressure on the accelerator. Tell your pupil to think of it as though pushing the car uphill, they would need a little more muscle and puff to get it to move, hence more acceleration.

At stage 5 many people lose the biting point as they release the hand brake: this is caused by inadvertently pushing the clutch in a little as they struggle with the hand brake. To counteract this, advise your pupil, once having pushed the release button in on the hand brake, to check again the clutch is still at biting position before lowering the hand brake lever.

Always remind your pupil that once the hand brake is released it is necessary to apply a little more acceleration before gently lifting up the clutch the rest of the way.

Rolling back
Rolling back is caused by:

- not having engaged first gear, or
- losing the biting point.

Mirror and shoulder checks are very important at the last moment before pulling away from the kerb.

Changing gears on a hill
When changing from first to second gear on a hill be careful that your driver does not change too soon. The car loses momentum very quickly on a hill, therefore a new driver may find that while changing gear they could roll to a halt. It's best if they wait until they are moving a bit faster than usual before going into second gear.

Be careful that your learner does not keep the foot on the clutch a second longer than necessary when travelling down a hill, otherwise the vehicle will start to coast. (Coasting, you should explain, happens when the clutch is pushed in too early and the car free wheels.)

SIGNALLING

Your pupil's aims will be to:

- understand **when** to signal, and **why** we signal
- understand the importance of **look** before signal
- know when to cancel signal
- know the correct signal to give
- understand the importance of brake lights when slowing down or stopping
- understand why they must check that other road users have reacted to their signal.

Using the indicators correctly
There are five main points for your pupil to remember when signalling:

1. Not signalling too early when there are many side roads: a signal applied too early could confuse drivers waiting to pull out.

2. When signalling to overtake stationary vehicles in town, it is advisable to cancel the indicator when you are at your furthest point to the right. This clarifies you are only overtaking, not turning right.

3. Always check the mirror **before** you signal, then check the mirror again before you change direction.

4. The idea of indicating is to inform other road users that you **intend** to change direction. **Don't** leave the indicator until you are actually moving out – this is dangerous.

5. Always ensure you give the correct signal at the correct time.

Hand signals
- Never give illegal signals, for example, waving someone on.
- A slowing down hand signal may be useful when stopping at a pedestrian crossing. However, **do not wave a pedestrian to come on**.

Brake lights
It is vital that your pupil learns to look well ahead and act on seeing brake lights come on. Brake lights give an early warning to cars behind that you are slowing down or stopping, hence in fast moving traffic it is important to be aware of the effect of braking on other traffic.

UNDERSTANDING SIGN LANGUAGE

A range of different roads and traffic conditions are ideal for this exercise, so that your learner can see as wide a variety of signs as possible. Initially this exercise should be carried out in daylight: night practice should come later.

Your pupil's aims will be to:

- be able to read the road
- understand road signs and the actions to take
- understand the difference between:
  - signs that warn
  - signs that inform
  - signs that give a positive order
  - signs that give a negative order

- understand various markings on the road
- understand the rules and signs at level crossings
- know and understand the sequence of traffic lights
- read and react correctly to Apache arrows (sharp deviation signs).

Understanding sign language

Forward planning and anticipation are the key to good, safe driving, therefore it is very important that a new driver reads, understands and reacts correctly to the signs they will see on the road.

The large numbers of signs can prove very confusing to the new driver; however, do explain that signs are not there to decorate the sides of the road, they cost a lot of money to produce and are there to warn or inform drivers about what lies ahead.

Explain the purpose of each sign, for example:

- **red rings** or circles give a **negative** instruction, such as:
  - No overtaking
  - No stopping
  - No entry

- **blue** circles give a positive instruction, such as:
  - You **must** turn right
  - You **must** travel at 30 mph or more.

Point out areas that have no signs *eg* unmarked crossroads, country lanes, new housing estates, and show the pupil the dangers.

Explain what a box junction is, and why we have them (to keep the flow of traffic moving at busy crossroads).

Explain the purpose of the reflective coloured studs – white, red and amber – which are on motorways and busy roads.

CHECKLIST

At the end of this session check that your pupil understands:
- how to move off on a hill without moving back
- what to do if they stall the car
- when to change gear and how to change smoothly
- how to read road signs correctly
- the importance of brake lights
- how and when to signal.

QUESTIONS AND ANSWERS

Q *Normally my pupil has no trouble on a hill start; however, on a very steep hill he finds difficulty releasing the hand brake. When he eventually manages he starts to roll back because he has lost the biting point while struggling with the hand brake. How can I correct this?*

A Suggest he tries lifting the hand brake up a little to press the release button and holding the hand there while he engages biting point; it is then just a matter of releasing the hand brake when he is ready to move. Encourage him to double check he is still at biting point after releasing the button on the hand brake as often the movement of hand can alter the balance of one's foot on the clutch, and the important biting point is lost. Always remind your student that a little more acceleration is needed just as he releases the hand brake. This coordination of feet and hands requires a lot of patience and practice.

Q *I am rather confused about signals: I lived in Germany for a number of years where the law states you must always signal if you are moving out or in, for example when you are going to overtake a vehicle and again when you move back in. However, when I took my English test I failed for unnecessary use of signals – why?*

A According to the manual *Driving*, which is the guidelines laid down by the Department of Transport, a signal might not be necessary when there is no one to benefit from it, or where the signal could confuse other road users. An example would be when you are overtaking a stationery vehicle, when able to move out gently in plenty of time and maintain a steady course. Always remember to check your mirrors before any change in direction.

Q *Is it true that until they pass the driving test all learners must go down each gear, not do block changes from fourth to second gear?*

A It is important to be in the correct gear for the situation in hand, which in today's busy traffic conditions often means it is quicker and safer to brake to adjust to the correct speed and go directly from fourth to second gear when the occasion arises. The more one has two hands on the wheel the safer it is, therefore unnecessary changing from say fifth to fourth to third to second to come to a stop would introduce untold hazards. An examiner is assessing whether a candidate can handle a car safely with due consideration for other road users; they don't expect them to drive like a novice.

CASE STUDIES

Julie helps get Susan up the hill

Julie was finding difficulty in explaining to Susan how to keep the biting point while checking the mirror and shoulder before moving out. The slightest movement of Susan's body resulted in a loss of the important bite.

'The more we tried the more frustrated we both felt. She was doing everything perfectly if it was a straight move off on a hill at a junction: however, if we were parked on a hill and Susan needed to check her shoulder for cyclists or cars passing before the final pull out, the movement caused the loss of bite.'

Julie decided to take over the driving seat for a little while and explain exactly what she did in the same circumstances. She found this more difficult than she expected as every movement she made was normally automatic, so analysing and explaining took more time than she anticipated.

'I eventually realised what I did was not have the full bite until the last second before I lowered the hand brake. We exchanged seats again and I asked Susan to get ready for her hill pull out with her clutch at the biting point, check her mirror, lift the hand brake up a little to release the button, then check the shoulder at this point. Then I asked her to accelerate a little and lift the clutch a fraction more to double check her biting point. She then lowered the hand brake. It worked!'

Philip encounters an unexpected problem

As Tessa had no problem when Philip explained hill starts, each pull out was perfect.

'You're a natural driver,' Philip remarked.

However, he soon regretted his words and could feel himself getting tense as they drove along. Tessa seemed to lose too much acceleration when she changed from first gear to second on a hill. She either came to a halt, or kept the car in first gear to the top of the hill, which sounded awful.

'I feel I don't have enough time to do everything,' said Tessa. 'I am delighted I pull away on the hill well: however, as soon as I start to change into second gear, the car starts to slow down too much, and by the time I'm in second I either start to kangaroo or come to a complete halt, and have to quickly use my foot brake to stop rolling back.'

After a lot of thought Philip decided to get Tessa to practise more stops and starts and moving up through the gears on a more level road, so she was able to change gear more quickly.

'Once I felt she was changing gears as smoothly and quickly as I normally do, we went back to this hill which we had been having trouble on,' said Philip.

Before Tessa pulled out Philip said, 'Now, Tessa, you have had no problems with going from first to second gear, so relax and just do what you have done previously; however, this time because we are on a hill I want you to count to six slowly before you try to change into second gear.'

Philip was delighted when his efforts were rewarded with a smooth drive up the hill.

Thomas gets the *Highway Code* out

Thomas found taking his brother Martin out was no problem initially: he handled the car well and was full of confidence. However, after a while he realised that Martin was not reading the road correctly.

'Why are the lines in the centre of the road of different lengths?' he asked Martin.

'To divide the road, and stop you falling asleep at the wheel,' replied Martin.

Thomas realised that Martin had not even read the *Highway Code*, so they decided that there would be no more lessons until he had studied it. Their next trip out was much better. 'I realise now what a difference it makes when someone reads the road correctly, acting on all the signs, adjusting the speed of the car, and observing generally,' said Thomas. 'I thought Martin was a confident driver, but seeing the difference in his driving now makes me realise he was just driving at speed without really being aware of the dangers around him.'

DISCUSSION POINTS

1. How important is it to make sure your student is in the correct gear at the correct time?

2. Accompanying a learner driver can be very stressful; after how long should you stop and have a break?

3. Teaching someone a skill always makes one analyse one's own ability. Do you feel your own driving is better, and you are more tolerant of other learner drivers now?

4
Driving under Control
round Bends and Corners

STEERING
Initially it's a good idea to keep to fairly quiet roads, main rather than non classified, as these will normally have clear road markings. When you start on right turns, the position for waiting to turn right will be clearly marked and protected by chevrons, thus giving your learner more confidence. It is also easier for other drivers to pass than on a narrow road, again taking pressure off your learner. This should be practised initially in daylight.

Your pupil's aims will be to:

- adjust speed using foot brake when necessary
- select the correct gear for the situation
- maintain control of the vehicle
- anticipate correctly the nature of the bend or corner
- avoid cutting corners or swinging out
- hold the steering wheel correctly
- anticipate hazards at all times.

Adjusting speed
The correct adjustment of speed is very important to learn at an early stage; remind your learner:

- never to accelerate into a bend, but ease off the accelerator slightly
- once round the bend and able to see the road in front you can accelerate out of the bend
- that the driver must have complete control of the vehicle throughout.

Selecting gears
Remind your learner to be in the correct gear in the correct position on the road at the correct time. Also point out:

- the sharper the bend, the lower the gear
- never change gear while turning the steering wheel.

Anticipating the nature of the bend

Help your learner to read the road correctly in order to anticipate the nature of any bends by:

- observing the traffic signs for bends and curves
- noticing how the telegraph poles are positioned in the distance
- looking for line markers in the centre of the road – the longer the line the greater the hazard
- noting the camber of the road.

Encourage your learner to anticipate other dangers which could be around the bend, such as:

- cyclists
- pedestrians
- horse riders
- road works
- slow-moving vehicles
- object in the road dropped by a previous vehicle
- accident
- a vehicle parked or broken down.

NEGOTIATING LEFT AND RIGHT TURNS

Industrial or housing estates are ideal for this kind of practice in the early stages. Try to find an area where children are not playing, and where there are plenty of left and right turns.

Your pupil's aims will be to:

- anticipate hazards around the corner
- select the correct gear for turning
- approach at the correct speed
- position the car correctly before the turn
- understand PSL (Position Speed Look)
- judge the right time to turn
- practise and understand MSM (Mirror Signal Manoeuvre)
- assess the type of junction.

Making left turns

Positioning
- The car should not be too close to the kerb as your learner turns,

about half a metre is a good guide. If your learner is too close to the kerb then the rear wheels could mount the kerb as you turn the corner.

• Explain the differences on approach to sharp and rounded bends: a sharp bend requires more pull and push on the steering wheel, on a rounded corner it is much easier to turn.

• Remind your learner that the slower the car is travelling, the lower the gear should be.

• Watch that your learner does not swing out to the right before turning.

Types of junctions
• Explain the difference between and the dangers of Y and T junctions.
• Explain the advantages of slip roads.
• Help your learner to read the road by pointing out how to assess the various types of junctions as you approach, *eg* traffic lights, stop, give way, priority.

Making right turns
Before starting on right turns draw a sketch to help your learner to understand the reason for positioning the car correctly for a right turn (see Figures 5 and 6). Initially, if possible find a right turn which has a marked area. This will help give your learner confidence.

Your pupil's aims will be to:

• understand the importance of correct positioning on approach
• use the mirror correctly
• judge correctly the speed of oncoming traffic
• wait to turn in the correct place in the road
• turn at the correct time
• be in the correct gear for the turn
• understand the advantages of marked areas for right turns ('cuddle in' places)
• know the dangers of:
  – bad positioning
  – cutting corners
  – swans neck

– waiting too far to the left or right
– cyclists
– pedestrians and traffic in new road.

Correct use of mirror
Remind your learner always to:

- check the mirror before indicating as a vehicle may have already indicated to overtake, or be in the process of passing

- check the mirror before any change of direction – the learner may have checked seconds before, but must remember that a car travelling at 60 miles an hour is moving 18 metres a second so in ten seconds a vehicle which was not even in rear vision has travelled 180 metres.

Correct positioning
Remind your learner:

- after indicating to take a gentle course toward the right hand side of their side of the road, being careful not to move too sharply to the right

- not to cross the centre reservation (centre of road) until actually turning – remember the right hand lane is for oncoming traffic

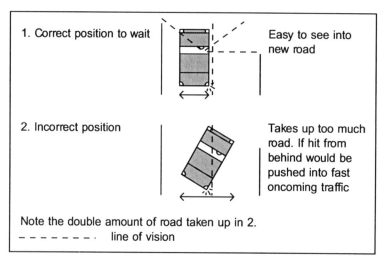

Fig. 5. Where to wait when turning right.

- when waiting to turn right the driver must position the vehicle to take up the minimum amount of space so as not to be a hazard to cars passing on the inside, or to oncoming vehicles.

- The correct position on a normal road is parallel to the centre white lines. By being in this position your learner will only take up the amount of road which is the width of the car. If they stop at an angle learners are doubling this, and also putting themselves in a dangerous position by having corners jutting into the path of vehicles passing on the inside plus most likely part of the front of the car is over the white line and in the path of oncoming cars (see Figure 5).

The best way to describe the correct waiting position to a new driver is for the driver to draw an imaginary line from the centre line of the road to be entered: the area behind where this crosses the centre line of the road the car is now on is where the driver is going to have to wait. (See Figure 6.)

Explain the danger of turning when you have passed this point. It would make it very difficult to turn into the new road without doing a 'swans neck' (going too far forward past the new junction as they turn), causing a very dangerous situation.

Warn your student to be careful not to move to the left once having indicated right: once the student has indicated an intention to turn right, cars behind can pass on the inside.

Be careful that your student does not try to rush a right turn, turning too early and cutting the corner.

USING MIRRORS CORRECTLY

Always remind your learner to keep an eye on what is happening behind by using the mirror correctly: someone could be overtaking just as the learner is entering a bend, so the learner must be prepared not to get involved in someone else's accident.

The six main points to emphasise to our learner are:

1. Drive according to your vision, never accelerate into an unknown.
2. Look well ahead.
3. Know what is happening on all four sides of the car.
4. Never set your internal mirror so that you have to move your head to look in it; it should be set so that you just move your eyes

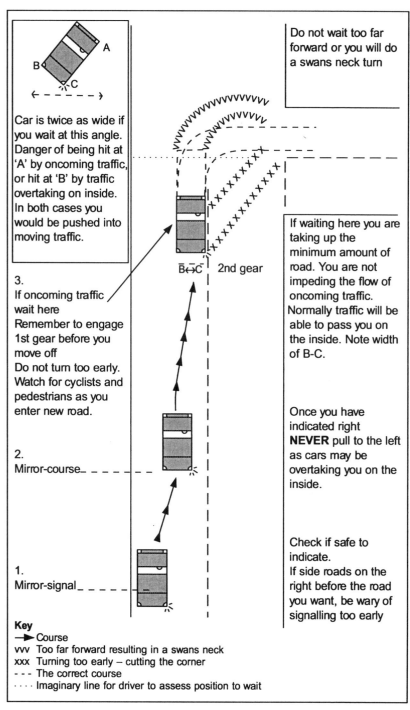

Do not wait too far forward or you will do a swans neck turn

A

B

C

Car is twice as wide if you wait at this angle. Danger of being hit at 'A' by oncoming traffic, or hit at 'B' by traffic overtaking on inside. In both cases you would be pushed into moving traffic.

B↔C   2nd gear

If waiting here you are taking up the minimum amount of road. You are not impeding the flow of oncoming traffic. Normally traffic will be able to pass you on the inside. Note width of B-C.

3.
If oncoming traffic wait here
Remember to engage 1st gear before you move off
Do not turn too early. Watch for cyclists and pedestrians as you enter new road.

Once you have indicated right **NEVER** pull to the left as cars may be overtaking you on the inside.

2.
Mirror-course

Check if safe to indicate.
If side roads on the right before the road you want, be wary of signalling too early

1.
Mirror-signal

Key
→ Course
vvv Too far forward resulting in a swans neck
xxx Turning too early – cutting the corner
- - - The correct course
· · · · Imaginary line for driver to assess position to wait

Fig. 6. Turning right.

46

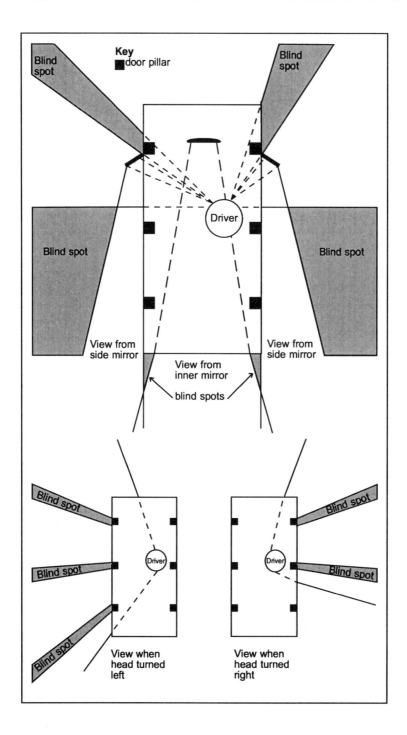

Fig. 7. Blind spots.

from looking ahead to the mirror.
5. Take a quick look in the mirror, then eyes back on the road ahead: never stare into the rear view mirror.
6. Use external mirrors to check for cyclists passing on the inside, particularly when turning left, or slowing down to stop.

Figure 7 shows the blind spots in all-round vision which your pupil should be aware of.

CHECKLIST

At the end of this session your learner should be able to:

● drive along normal roads safely
● do left turns correctly
● turn right, understanding the dangers of incorrect positioning
● understand and act correctly at all road signs and road markings.

QUESTIONS AND ANSWERS

Q *What are the main dangers at Y junctions?*

A At Y junctions it is often more difficult to see traffic coming from your right, also when turning right you have to be careful of your positioning.

Q *When turning from a main road into a minor road what are the principal dangers to look for?*

A People crossing the road, cyclists, children, parked cars, road works.

Q *If I am turning right off a main road and someone coming towards me is also turning right, what do we do?*

A Unless road markings dictate otherwise you pass behind the oncoming car and he passes behind you, off side to off side. This way you both have maximum vision before the final turn.

CASE STUDIES

Julie cures Susan's nerves
When they started doing right turns on roads with more traffic, Julie

found that if Susan had to stop and wait for oncoming traffic, she would stall the car on moving off when the road was clear.

'I found that the more nervous she became, because of the stalling, plus waiting for oncoming traffic, the more worried I became, having to wait so long in such an exposed part of the road,' Julie said. She therefore decided to go back to square one.

'We went back to really quiet roads where there was just an occasional car to wait for, building up Susan's confidence and improving her speed in observation and selecting her gear quickly. We also sat and discussed the approach to right turns on a main road and the advantages of good positioning. We then tried the road again where previously we had had all the trouble. I was a little apprehensive as we approached the right turn,' Julie said. 'However, I managed to keep myself relaxed and reminded Susan as we approached to keep planning ahead, use her mirrors, gears and to get in the right position. When she had to stop for oncoming traffic, she immediately selected first gear, and moved off smoothly as soon as the road was clear. We were both delighted. I think the secret is not to rush your student.'

Philip finds a way of seeing round parked cars

Philip was pleased that Tessa was doing so well with her driving, but they encountered a problem when coming to a junction where several parked cars blocked their view down the road they were turning into.

'We really couldn't see a thing,' said Philip. 'I suggested that Tessa tried to pull forward a little more, but we still couldn't see the traffic on the road we were trying to enter. It didn't help that the traffic on this other road was moving fast, and a van had parked right on the corner.'

Philip tried to think of a way to help Tessa to get a better view of the pull out.

'If you think about it, Tessa,' he eventually said, 'We have stopped at the end of our road, moved forward a little and still cannot see; however, all the vehicles on the road we are pulling out into are taking a course to overtake all those stationery vehicles. Therefore we are safe to move slowly forward, just creeping until the front of our car is on a line with the parked car which is furthest into the road. Our vision will then be much clearer, and we can use this as our position for waiting.'

Tessa slowly eased the car forward until she was able to see clearly down the road she wanted to enter.

Thomas lays down the law

Martin was rushing his driving to such an extent that on right turns he repeatedly cut corners. In the end Thomas decided to pull Martin in a quiet part of the road; he then got out the booklet *The Driving Test*, and found the page which showed 'Crossing the path of other vehicles'.

'Read that, and digest it,' he said. 'I don't intend to waste an afternoon taking you out if you repeatedly ignore what I am trying to explain to you. You are putting our lives and other people at risk. This is not a speedway – you must show more consideration for other road users when driving.'

After discussing what it said in the book, they returned to practising right turns without any more problems.

DISCUSSION POINTS

1. List five major dangers to look out for when turning right.

2. How would you explain the importance of the *Highway Code* to your learner?

3. Do you find after instructing a learner that you are more considerate about where and how you park?

5
Coping with More Complex Roads

Before taking your learner onto more complex roads where they are going to encounter a lot of fast traffic, impatient and intolerant drivers, and will need to think quickly, it is important to make sure that they are confident with the basics of driving: the use of gears, the correct coordination of clutch and accelerator, and most important the understanding and correct use of mirrors and forward observation.

COPING WITH TRAFFIC LIGHTS

Traffic lights are perhaps most worrying for a learner. They feel pressurised to be 'quick off the mark', often resulting in a stall, or even trying to rush the lights. If just as the lights turn to green, someone behind impatiently sounds the horn, it can result in such tension, even panic, in your learner, that a stall is inevitable. Therefore extra patience is required on the part of the accompanying driver who must encourage the learner to ignore the offending impatient driver and concentrate on negotiating the junction.

You might find it useful to remind your learner that if they were being served in a shop and the person behind shouted for them to hurry up, other people would think the impatient person either very rude or mentally ill: there would be no reason to rush the transaction in any way.

Try and find a route which encounters different types of light-controlled junctions, both busy, and quiet, and also pelican crossing lights.

Your pupil's aims will be to:

- approach traffic lights correctly
- know who has priority
- anticipate the actions of pedestrians and cyclists
- use the mirror correctly

- move off smoothly when safe to do so
- wait in the correct place when turning right and there is oncoming traffic
- know the correct sequence of traffic lights and their meaning
- understand why at some lights there is a yellow box junction
- act correctly at lights with box junctions
- appreciate the important of alertness at all times.

Approaching traffic lights

Early anticipation of the nature of the junction is important, so your student should be:

- looking well ahead on approach
- noting the type of junction
- aware of the volume of traffic going each way
- noting the colour of the lights ahead
- anticipating the colour the lights will be on arrival at the junction.

Make sure your student knows the sequence of traffic lights: it helps to keep traffic flowing steadily when a driver is aware what comes after each colour or combination of colours. Starting with the green light the sequence is:

- Green: you can proceed if safe to do so.
- Amber: stop at the stop line – you can proceed only if you have already crossed the stop line.
- Red: do not cross the stop line – stop and wait for the lights to return to green.
- Red and amber together: also means stop; however, it also indicates that the next colour will be green, so be prepared to move away when the lights turn to green.

Understanding priority at lights

Students often get confused about who has priority at traffic lights. It can help them if you explain that all the lights are doing is changing which way the main road runs. When your lights are on green, your road now becomes the major road, and as on all major roads if you are proceeding straight ahead you can if it's safe to do so; however, if you are going to turn left or right, you then have to think of the various dangers: cyclists, pedestrians, other vehicles *etc.*

- Remind your student that green does not give you overall priority,

it just means proceed if safe to do so.
- Make sure your student is aware that pedestrian lights could be on green in the roads to the right and left.

Mirrors and observation
Make sure your student:

- frequently checks the mirrors on approach and always before any change in direction
- is always aware of the dangers of drivers who are 'amber gamblers'
- stops smoothly, aware at all times of the traffic behind.

Using box junctions
A box junction is designed to help the flow of traffic and consists of crisscross yellow lines. Remind your student that he/she:

- must not enter the box until the exit is clear
- may stop in the box if wanting to turn right and is prevented from doing so by the flow of oncoming traffic
- knows not to enter the box if there is a traffic hold up ahead, even if the lights are on green.

Turning to the right or left
The same rules apply when turning at traffic lights as on a normal road. Your pupil must look out for

- cyclists passing on the inside when the vehicle is turning left
- pedestrians crossing the road the vehicle wants to enter
- parked cars or buses stopping round the corner
- oncoming traffic when the vehicle is turning right.

Giving way at pelican crossings
At pelican crossings the red and amber light is replaced by an amber flashing light. When this is flashing drivers must give way to pedestrians, when the light turns to green drivers must check that all pedestrians have cleared the crossing before proceeding.

DRIVING ON DUAL CARRIAGEWAYS

Dual carriageways usually carry much faster moving traffic: it is therefore advisable to help your learner understand the additional hazards of driving on this type of road. Do ensure your learner is confident with left and right turns in traffic before attempting them on dual carriageways, as a slow or hesitant learner could be a potential hazard in the fast flow of traffic.

Your pupil's aims will be to:

- understand how to change lanes correctly
- use side mirrors correctly
- expand awareness of dangers around the vehicle
- negotiate left and right turns off a dual carriageway
- enter a dual carriageway correctly without impeding the flow of traffic.

Changing lanes

When there is fast moving traffic it is more important than normal to plan well ahead any change in direction: if you want to overtake a bicycle, or pass a parked car or any other obstacle, it is important to check the mirror and inform following traffic in plenty of time by indicating. On some occasions an early and smooth course can be taken without indicating; however, your learner should be aware of the risk of cars in the blind spot of their mirrors (Figure 7), so must practise extra observation.

Side mirrors

Using side mirrors, and being aware that they can make a vehicle look further away than it really is, is an essential exercise in learning to drive a car. An extra check in both mirrors before changing lanes is essential, and is good practice for the future when your newly qualified driver can drive on motorways. (In Great Britain it is forbidden for learner drivers to drive on a motorway.)

> Remind your learner that it is important to know what is happening at all times on all four sides of the vehicle.

Turning off a dual carriageway to the left

When turning off a dual carriageway it is important to inform following cars of your intention in plenty of time using the indicator; however, your pupil must be very careful not to indicate too early especially if there are numerous side roads to the left, as traffic waiting to pull onto the road may think the car is turning, and pull out causing an accident.

Tell your pupil that its best to wait until having passed the entrance to the last side road on the left before the one they need before indicating. Be careful that your pupil does not pull to the right before a left turn.

Heavy vehicle and bus drivers often indicate left and pull over to the right to enable them to negotiate their large vehicle into the side road. Make sure your pupil knows never to overtake on the inside thinking they have used the wrong indicator.

Turning right off a dual carriageway

Many dual carriageways have signs which forbid right or 'U' turns, so it is important for your learner to read all signs to ensure that it is permitted to turn right. If there is a special lane for vehicles turning right, make sure your learner changes lanes and enters it at the earliest opportunity. When there is no special lane and your learner has to stop for oncoming vehicles, make sure the learner waits in a safe position without the vehicle jutting into the fast lanes of both carriageways.

Remind your learner that oncoming traffic could be travelling very fast, and warn of the dangers of other drivers giving illegal signals, *eg* waving you on. Your learner must be aware that while an oncoming driver might be willing to let you pull out, the other vehicles don't know this and will still be passing – often in the learner's blind spot.

Crossing a dual carriageway

When approaching a dual carriageway from a side road impress upon your pupil that much care must be taken before pulling out, especially if needing to cross to a road opposite. Remind the learner of these points:

- If bushes, trees, parked vehicles or even pedestrians obstruct the learner's vision, move slowly forward a few inches to improve his/her view of the moving traffic.

- If there is a wide centre reservation where it is safe to wait without restricting the flow of traffic on the dual carriageway, once it is safe to move forward the learner can wait to complete the crossing in this area.

- If the centre reservation is not wide enough the learner should not emerge from a side road until all lanes are clear.

- If in any doubt **wait**.

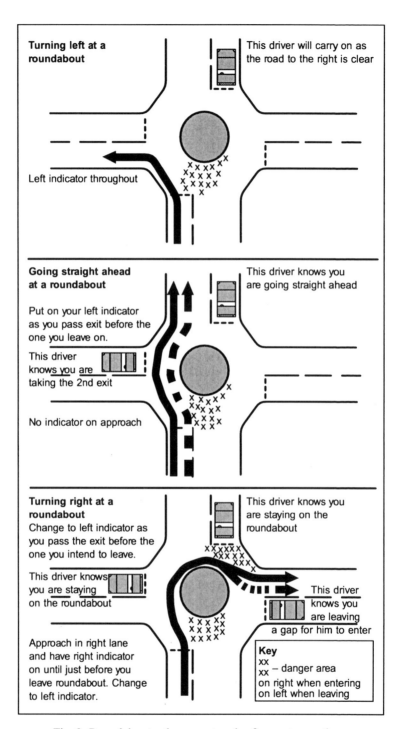

Turning left at a roundabout

This driver will carry on as the road to the right is clear

Left indicator throughout

Going straight ahead at a roundabout

This driver knows you are going straight ahead

Put on your left indicator as you pass exit before the one you leave on.

This driver knows you are taking the 2nd exit

No indicator on approach

Turning right at a roundabout
Change to left indicator as you pass the exit before the one you intend to leave.

This driver knows you are staying on the roundabout

This driver knows you are staying on the roundabout

This driver knows you are leaving a gap for him to enter

Approach in right lane and have right indicator on until just before you leave roundabout. Change to left indicator.

Key
xx
xx – danger area
on right when entering
on left when leaving

Fig. 8. Roundabouts: the correct and safe way to use them.

NEGOTIATING ROUNDABOUTS

A roundabout is normally at a busy junction and allows traffic to flow more quickly, merging and flowing from different directions. When taking your pupils to roundabouts at the early stages try to use large ones rather than mini ones, as it will be easier for them to understand the flow and the danger areas.

Your pupil's aims will be to:

- know the type of roundabout on approach
- understand the danger areas when entering and leaving a roundabout
- select the correct lane when approaching a roundabout
- be in the correct gear at the correct time
- approach at the correct speed
- use the indicators correctly
- understand how to negotiate the roundabout safely.

Approaching a roundabout

It is very important to plan well ahead when approaching a roundabout, observing any special road markings. The majority of roundabouts in the UK give priority to vehicles already on the roundabout; however, some have different rules, so it is important to read the signs on approach.

Your student should be aware of the following points:

- To take the first exit off the roundabout, approach in the left lane with the left indicator flashing. Keep to the left hand lane on the roundabout.

- To go straight ahead at the roundabout, approach in the left lane, as if approaching a cross roads to go directly ahead. Keep to the left lane on the roundabout. Be extra observant on approach as there may be road markings dictating that drivers should approach in the second lane if going straight ahead. While on the roundabout there is no need to operate the indicator until just before the desired exit.

- To take the third exit from the roundabout, or any exit past the second, indicate right on approach and negotiate the roundabout in the right hand lane near the centre reservation. Change to the left indicator once you have passed the exit before the one you are going to leave on.

- On entering a roundabout the danger area is on the right. It's a good idea for your learner to think of it as entering a normal main road.

Leaving a roundabout

Having successfully entered the roundabout, the next manoeuvre is to leave it. Make sure your pupil remembers:

- When leaving a roundabout the danger area is on the left. Be aware of traffic which may be on the inside, especially cyclists.
- Indicate left immediately on passing the exit just before the one intended.
- On leaving the roundabout look ahead for any dangers in the new road.
- Use mirrors and all round observation throughout the operation.

CHECKLIST

At the end of this session your learner should be able to:

- approach traffic lights correctly
- understand how to drive on a dual carriageway safely and how to cross it
- negotiate a roundabout.

QUESTIONS AND ANSWERS

Q *I get a bit muddled at mini roundabouts, especially when there is a double mini roundabout. How should I negotiate them?*

A You approach in the same way as a normal roundabout; however, there is less space and time to signal and manoeuvre. On double mini roundabouts don't enter the first roundabout until you are sure that you can enter and exit from the second without stopping or interfering with the progress of other traffic.

Q *Why do you indicate to leave a roundabout?*

A To help the person waiting to enter the roundabout: when he sees you are indicating to leave he knows he can enter into the space you are going to leave. It is very important not to indicate too early and thereby imply you are leaving by an earlier exit.

Q *Why when turning right at a roundabout do you keep your right indicator going until just before your exit?*

A This clarifies to other road users exactly where you are going, helping traffic waiting to enter know that you will be staying on the roundabout to pass at least one other exit.

CASE STUDIES

Julie gets the green light
Julie's pupil Susan was repeatedly slowing down far too soon on approach to traffic lights, annoying following traffic.

'I'm making sure I can stop in time if the lights change,' Susan said.

Julie realised after a while that the major problem was that Susan didn't understand the sequence of lights.

'If you see it red on approach, and it's been red for a while, the chances are by the time you arrive at the lights it could be green, so you just need to look ahead, be prepared to stop if necessary; however, a small adjustment in speed nearer the junction may be all that is necessary,' Julie explained. 'If as you approach the lights they are on amber, you know that the next colour is going to be red, so approach them as you would a normal stop sign: there is no need to go right down to second gear as you are going to have to stop and wait for the lights to change.'

Once Julie explained the sequence of lights to Susan, she was able to approach the lights with greater confidence.

Philip finds that there is no magic roundabout
Philip was starting to feel really relaxed when taking Tessa for her regular driving practice, so much so that he decided she should take a turn at the wheel when they went on holiday. He was so relaxed with Tessa that he was not observing the road ahead himself, tending to rely on her observation too much, forgetting she was still learning. It was only when he heard the screech of brakes, and the blast of a horn, that Philip remembered that he was still very much responsible for Tessa's actions.

'You went straight over a mini roundabout,' he shouted at Tessa.

'Well, I didn't see anything,' Tessa replied, fighting back the tears of shock.

'You almost got us killed,' Philip replied angrily.

In the stony silence that followed Philip realised that he was wrong to blame Tessa: she was still a learner, and he had not explained about mini roundabouts as they didn't have any in their town. He should also have been more aware of the road ahead as he was responsible for her driving while accompanying her.

'Let's pull in and stop for a while and discuss this,' he said.

He explained about mini roundabouts, and they retraced their route to approach the junction with the mini roundabout again. This time both Philip and Tessa were looking and planning ahead.

Thomas moves the stop line

Once, when Thomas was taking Martin out for a lesson, they became caught up with the traffic going to a big football match as they tried to pull onto the dual carriageway from a side road with a stop.

'I can't see a thing,' Martin said when he stopped at the stop line. 'People have parked their cars on the dual carriageway.'

'You have stopped at the line, so you can slowly creep forward using your clutch to control your speed,' Thomas replied.

Martin moved slowly forward but still could not see past the parked vehicles, and the traffic was moving fast in the outside lane.

Thomas thought for a minute, trying to ignore the impatient drivers behind him, one of whom had already sounded his horn twice. What did he normally do in this sort of situation?

'Look, Martin,' he eventually said, 'pretend there is a stop line running along the outside of these parked cars: you can move as far forward as that without impeding the flow of traffic and your vision should be far better.'

They crept slowly forward a fraction at a time until the vision was better, and eventually eased into a gap in the traffic.

DISCUSSION POINTS

1. Most accidents happen within a radius of five miles of home – can you think why?

2. How long do you think a learner can drive before he starts to lose concentration?

3. Do you yourself use your mirrors enough when driving?

6
Manoeuvring the Car

The three manoeuvres which an examiner requires a candidate to be able to do are:

- reverse parking
- reversing round a corner
- turning in the road.

Candidates will be asked to do only two of the three in the driving test; however, the candidate must be able to do all three. In each case the examiner will be looking out for:

- all round observation at all times
- the ability to move the car slowly by using the clutch and accelerator correctly
- moving the car smoothly without jerking
- showing awareness and consideration at all times of other road users.

Before you start to teach any of the manoeuvres it's a good idea for your learner to practise moving slowly, using the clutch and brake as if in a traffic jam. Once your learner feels able to creep along at a snail's pace, it will give confidence for the manoeuvres.

TURNING IN THE ROAD

Teaching the turn in the road first can be useful as it incorporates all the manoeuvres and skills which are needed for the reverse and parking, and your learner will find it easier to do these when you are ready to teach them. Find a wide fairly quiet road to demonstrate and practise this manoeuvre. Demonstrate it twice to your learner before letting them try it. As you demonstrate drive very slowly, explaining exactly what you are doing, and why.

Your pupil's aims will be to:

- turn the car around in the road so it faces the opposite way
- be aware at all times what is happening on all four sides of the car
- know the dangers of the tail end of the car being over the pavement
- adjust the fine balance of the clutch and accelerator, particularly on the crown of the road.
- use the foot brake smoothly and correctly
- apply and release the hand brake at the correct time.

Your commentary on your demonstration should be on these lines:

The turn in the road: part 1

1. I am stopping in a suitable place in the road, making sure I am not blocking a driveway or going to be worried by parked cars on the opposite side of the road when I move forward. I am also checking to see if there are any trees, lamp posts or bollards just in front of the car, to which I would have to pay particular attention when I come to the reverse part of this manoeuvre, because of the overhanging tail of the car. If as I reverse, there is a tree or lamp post directly behind my rear window, it also cuts down the amount of space in which I have to manoeuvre in.

2. I am now engaging first gear and checking all round to make sure there aren't any vehicles, cyclists or pedestrians.

3. As I let off my hand brake, I lift up the clutch a fraction so I am just moving, *creeping* along.

4. I am turning the steering wheel smoothly and quickly to the right, still keeping my feet balanced on the clutch and accelerator, perhaps needing a little more acceleration as I near the crown of the road.

5. Note that I am still looking in all directions as I move in case there are any elderly people, children or dogs who may appear in the area.

6. As I go over the brow of the road I need to ease off slightly on the accelerator as the camber is now causing the car to move slightly downhill.

7. As I near the kerb I start to turn the wheel to the left to straighten the wheels and prepare for the next part of the manoeuvre.

8. I move my foot off the accelerator and onto the foot brake to come to a smooth stop just before the kerb, being careful not to roll into the gutter.

9. I now apply the hand brake before getting reading for the second part of the manoeuvre.

At this stage you should explain how all round observation is important before starting the second part of the manoeuvre. Show the need to check what is happening on all four sides of the car, and ensure your student understands the importance of waiting longer if necessary, if any traffic is in view. Particular attention must be made to looking out the back window, not just using the mirror to see out.

The turn in the road: part 2

1. After checking it is safe to continue with my manoeuvre I now engage reverse gear; remembering that all roads have a camber, I shall be reversing slightly uphill, therefore I make sure my clutch is at the biting point before I release the hand brake.

2. Looking behind, because this is the way I am travelling, checking either side for other road users, I move slowly, turning my wheel briskly to the left, as this will move the rear of the car to the left.

3. Note my foot is on the clutch at all times: if I feel I am moving a little too fast then I can push the clutch in a fraction. Again as I go over the brow of the road I may need to adjust the position of my feet on the clutch and accelerator slightly.

4. Once I am over the brow I start to turn the wheel in the opposite direction, which is to the right, to straighten the wheels and prepare them for the next part of the manoeuvre.

5. I am now slowing down to stop, checking both sides and behind me to make sure I don't travel too far back and hit the kerb, or allow the overhang of the boot to hinder passing pedestrians or hit a tree or lamp post.

6. I now come to a gentle stop using my foot brake. I then apply my hand brake.

Do emphasise that you always stop with the foot brake keeping two hands firmly on the wheel, then apply the hand brake.

It's worth pointing out that when travelling backwards you look to the back of the car and turn the wheel the way you want the back of the car to go; the same as when travelling forward you look forward and turn the wheel the way you want the front of the car to travel. Although this may seem very basic it does take away the fear that learners have when learning to reverse.

The turn in the road: part 3

1. Again checking for any traffic, pedestrians or cyclists on both sides of the car, I engage first gear, remembering because of the camber of the road to ensure my clutch is at the biting point before releasing the hand brake.

2. I am pulling the wheel briskly to the right as this is the way I want the front of the car to travel.

3. Again I may need a slight adjustment to my accelerator and clutch as I go over the brow of the road.

4. I check my mirror and come to a stop alongside the kerb. I straighten the wheels by pulling the steering wheel slightly to the left.

5. Once stopped I apply the hand brake and then put the gear lever in neutral.

Do explain to your learner that the manoeuvre does not have to be carried out in three movements: if it is a narrow road then it is quite acceptable to go backwards and forwards again making it five manoeuvres.

Emphasise the importance of observation and clutch control in this exercise: it must always be carried out slowly, smoothly and with maximum observation on all sides of the car. It is dangerous to do it too fast.

Remember to always demonstrate this twice to your learner before asking them to try to do it. When your learner is trying it for the first time be extra patient and also extra observant not only of your learner but for any traffic or pedestrians. Once you have taught your learner the turn in the road, practise it at least once each time you go out for a lesson. Remember 'practice makes perfect'.

REVERSING ROUND A CORNER

Reversing, like the turn in the road, should be carried out slowly and with extra observation. Pedestrians, especially children, expect a car to be moving forward not backwards: observation therefore is very important when carrying out this manoeuvre. On a driving test the examiner will stop before the side road which he expects your learner to reverse into. This is to give the candidate a chance to look into the road he is going to reverse into, check on the type of reverse required and observe any dangers. It also gives the candidate an opportunity to position the car not too close to the kerb when moving forward to the point where they will start the manoeuvre.

Your pupil's aims will be to:

- move the vehicle backwards
- manipulate clutch and accelerator correctly to control the vehicle
- have suitable observation at all times
- apply reasonable accuracy.

Preparing to reverse round a corner

Stopping before the road which you want your learner to reverse into has a threefold advantage:

1. It gives the learner a chance to look into the road and to study the type of corner which he/she is going to reverse round.

2. It gives the learner an opportunity to practise stopping correctly at a suitable place, and to pull away from the kerb correctly, remembering to check over the shoulder before pulling out.

3. It enables the learner to position the car not too close to the kerb when moving forward to the place for starting the reverse.

The three main types of corners which your learner might be asked to reverse around are shown in Figure 9.

Moving backwards in a straight line

Before moving backwards it is very important that your learner checks all around to make sure it is safe to do so. The learner needs to check that:

- no cars are coming up behind
- no pedestrians are likely to be crossing the road behind

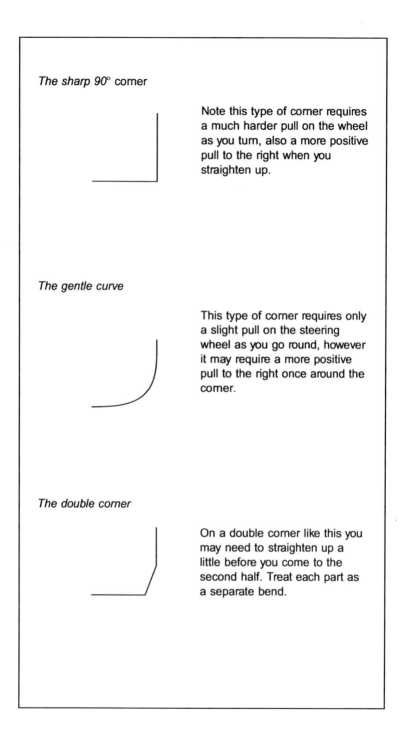

The sharp 90° corner

Note this type of corner requires a much harder pull on the wheel as you turn, also a more positive pull to the right when you straighten up.

The gentle curve

This type of corner requires only a slight pull on the steering wheel as you go round, however it may require a more positive pull to the right once around the corner.

The double corner

On a double corner like this you may need to straighten up a little before you come to the second half. Treat each part as a separate bend.

Fig.9. Types of corners.

- no cyclists are either behind or coming out of the road that the learner is going to reverse into
- no cars are waiting to pull out the side road which the learner wants to reverse into.

Once your learner has engaged reverse gear, remind him/her that as in the 'turn in the road', it is the clutch that is going to control the speed of the car, also when travelling backwards the learner should turn the body so as to be looking out the back window.

When the learner starts to travel backwards, which must be slowly, if a vehicle is seen coming up behind, explain that it is necessary to stop and wait for it to pass before continuing.

If the car starts to move towards the kerb, the learner needs to give a little pull on the steering wheel, to the right.

Negotiating the corner
When the rear of the car gets to the corner (this is when your learner loses sight of the corner in his rear window), the learner needs to start to pull the steering wheel to the left (the way he/she wants the rear of the car to go).

Your pupil must check all round that there are no vehicles or pedestrians before turning the wheel (it is best to stop for this check as it gives the learner more time to think).

Remind your learner that the front of the car will swing out into the road as the car reverses into the side road.

Once the learner is round the corner and can see the road clearly behind them, explain that he/she now needs to straighten the car by turning the wheel in the opposite direction (to the right). A slight feathering (turning a little to the left then to the right) might be necessary to arrive at the final position.

As the teacher, you must remember to explain to your learner:

- To stop before the road the vehicle is going to reverse into to enable your learner to look at the corner and position the vehicle not too close to the kerb.

- The importance of slowness, which makes it easier to correct mistakes and easier for observation. Remind your learner that this is all achieved by clutch control.

- To explain how the front of the car will swing out as you turn the corner, becoming twice its width as it turns.

Golden rules of reverse

1. *Observation*
   Always know what is happening all round your car, particularly before you start to turn the corner. Stop and have another look around if you feel at all unsure.

2. *Always travel very slowly*
   People don't expect cars to go backwards. Stop if you see a cyclist or another car.

3. *Always turn your steering wheel the way you want the car to go.*
   If you are too far away from the kerb pull towards the kerb. If you are too near, pull away.

4. *Look as far behind you as you can*
   Particularly when straightening up.

Position of vehicle when stopped
Not too close to kerb

Turn wheel to left when kerb cannot be seen in rear window.
Care in observation at this point as the front of the car will swing out as you turn the steering wheel to the left

Instructor to stop and give instructions at this point – check shoulder before pull out

Cars do not bend in middle so note at this point you will look miles away from the kerb

Look well back

Once vehicle is around corner, start to turn wheel to the right, before the rear of the car dips towards the kerb

Key
A – stop to look at road
B – stop to prepare for reverse
C – half way point
D - straightening up

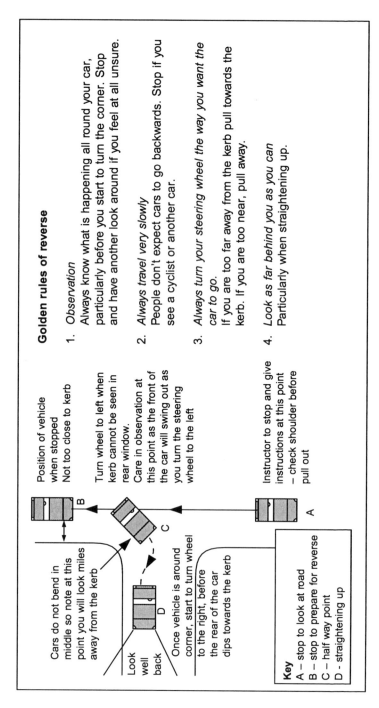

Fig. 10. Reversing round a corner.

- The importance of observation: stop if anything is approaching behind or coming towards you when about to turn into the corner.

- This manoeuvre has to be carried out with reasonable accuracy; however, this does not mean two inches from the kerb – about half a metre is quite acceptable.

- To remind your learner that if they feel they are getting too close to the kerb they can stop, go forward a little then carry on the reverse. After all, if they were going to reverse into a garage and thought their positioning was taking them into the door, they would not carry on, saying afterwards to their family, 'sorry, I have damaged the garage door and car, but I had started so had to finish'. The family would most likely think they needed medical help. To go forward and backwards again is not only the sensible thing to do, but also it takes the fear of making a mistake away from your learner.

- To explain that the same rules applies to vision going backwards as going forwards, always look well backwards down the road.

- To remind the learner that if they want the rear of the car to go to the left more (be nearer the kerb) they should turn the wheel to the left; if they want the rear to go to the right, they should turn the wheel to the right.

- To stress that your learner should never look forward and drive backwards, after all they wouldn't drive forwards looking out the back window! A quick glance forward to check for traffic is the only time it is feasible.

Learners often worry when, in the middle of the bend, they notice that both the rear and front seem far away from the kerb. Explain, using a plastic car, or even a pencil, that a rigid object going round a corner is 45° away from the corner at both front and rear ends at mid turn.

Practise this on as many different corners as you can to give your learner confidence.

REVERSE PARKING

This manoeuvre requires clutch control and observation similar to when doing the turn in the road and the reverse.

Your pupil's aims will be to:

- reverse and park the car
  - safely
  - behind a parked car
  - within the space of two cars
- stop reasonably close to the kerb
- avoid swinging from side to side or mounting the kerb
- show consideration at all times to other road users.

Preparing to reverse park the car
This exercise is best carried out in daylight in the initial stages. Find a quiet road with parked cars, ask your learner to stop so you can explain exactly what is required. Initially it is best to find a parked car which has at least four car lengths' space behind.

- Ask your learner to move forward and stop alongside the vehicle in front, not too close to it and not more than 1 metre away.

- Remember to make sure that your learner checks his mirror before pulling out.

- Explain to your learner the importance of clutch control in this exercise.

- Ask your learner to move back a little until the rear of your car is alongside the car you have stopped next to.

- Emphasise the importance of checking for passing and oncoming vehicles at this point, as when your learner starts to turn the wheel the front of the car will swing out into the road.

- Tell your learner that once the back of your car is on line with the rear of the car you are reversing behind, it is quite safe to start turning the wheel.

- Remind your learner that you always turn the wheel the way you want the rear of the car to go, so if the learner has stopped by a car on the left and intends to park behind it the learner needs to pull the wheel to the left.

- Stress the importance of keeping the clutch pedal steady so that your learner can move the car slowly and smoothly.

- Remember that your learner will need a slight left lock at this stage.

- Tell your learner to straighten up when the rear of the car is about a foot from the kerb or, if there is a vehicle behind, the learner can use its nearside headlamp as a guide to the best position to start straightening up.

- Warn your learner to watch carefully where the front of the car is before straightening up, making sure it is clear of the car in front otherwise there is a danger of clipping the corner of this car.

- Learners can get very worried at this point as they feel the front is at a bad angle, explain that the front of the car will move in when you do the final part of the manoeuvre.

- The learner now can move forward a little, pulling the wheel to the left to straighten the car and make the position look tidy.

CHECKLIST

At the end of this session your learner should understand:

- How to do the three manoeuvres which are:
  - the turn in the road
  - the reverse round a corner
  - parking behind a stationary car
- the importance of all round observation
- the correct use of the clutch to control the car at slow speeds.

QUESTIONS AND ANSWERS

Q *My major problem is trying to explain the straightening up at the end of a reverse. My pupil has no difficulty getting round a corner, however, as soon as he is round and the car looks straight, he then goes all over the place once he has to move backwards a little further. What can I do to help him solve this problem?*

A This is a problem encountered by many learner drivers – they presume because the car is now in a straight line they don't need to turn the steering any more. You must explain that, although the car looks straight, the front wheels of the car are at an angle

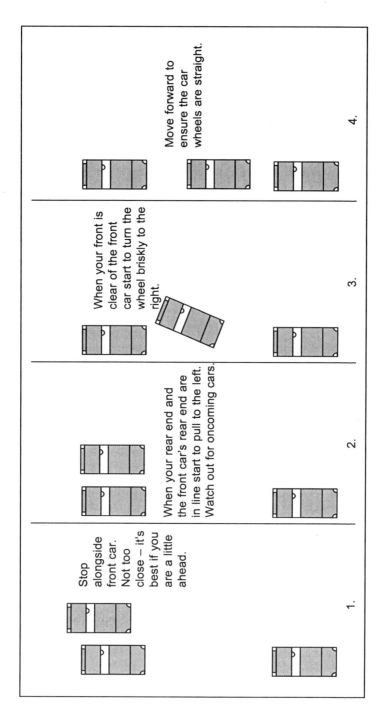

Fig. 11. Reverse parking.

1. Stop alongside front car. Not too close – it's best if you are a little ahead.

2. When your rear end and the front car's rear end are in line start to pull to the left. Watch out for oncoming cars.

3. When your front is clear of the front car start to turn the wheel briskly to the right.

4. Move forward to ensure the car wheels are straight.

still after negotiating the corner, therefore you need to straighten them up. Remind your learner that he has just pulled the steering wheel quite hard to the left therefore to get his wheels in a straight line a good firm couple of pulls to the right is necessary to get the front wheels of the car straight. Tell them to watch the rear left corner carefully and if it starts to move to the right give a gentle pull to the left to get it straight again.

Q *What is the best thing to do if I am teaching the reverse and a car appears in the side road I am going to reverse into?*

A At all times you must consider other road users and if you feel the person coming out from the side road is unsure of what you are doing move forward and start again.

Q *If we are in the middle of a turn in the road and a vehicle approaches and stops, I find my learner gets very nervous because they are now being watched. Should I wave the waiting vehicle on?*

A It is illegal to give unauthorised hand signals; you might wave a car to proceed and not notice another vehicle coming the other way. It's wisest to finish the part of the manoeuvre you are doing then just smile and nod at the waiting driver who usually will carry on when he considers it safe to do so.

CASE STUDIES

Julie discovers that 'even while they teach men learn'

Julie was not too happy about teaching Susan how to reverse park.

'To be honest I don't feel too confident myself about reversing into a parking place,' she admitted to Susan's mother. 'So I really don't know if I am going to be able to teach this.'

'I'm afraid I can't help you because I myself have never driven,' replied Mrs Gray. 'However, you have taught Susan everything else so well, and I am sure knowing the principles of what you are supposed to do must help in some way.'

Julie went home and thought about it. She was a confident driver, had no problem with normal reversing, but had this nervous feeling about parking between cars. As she thought about it she realised that she always felt she was causing a hold up whenever she tried to reverse park, therefore tried to hurry up. The next day Julie took Susan out to teach her how to reverse park.

'The secret,' Julie said, 'is not to rush it. You must use your clutch to go nice and slow so that you have plenty of time to look around for passing vehicles or pedestrians.'

At the first attempt Susan was turning too hard to the left and getting too close to the kerb before straightening up.

'Move forward and try again,' said Julie.

When the same thing happened again, Julie decided to demonstrate the correct amount of lock on the wheel. She was a little apprehensive as she took the driver's seat: 'I hope I don't make a mess of this,' she thought to herself. However, she carefully did a reverse park as explained in the book, letting Susan know exactly what she was doing, and was delighted with how easy she found it.

After Julie's demonstration, Susan was able to park much better, and Julie found that with each practice that Susan had, she herself became much more confident in her own ability to reverse park.

Philip gets angry

Philip had been trying to teach Tessa the reverse the last three times they had gone out for a practice drive. There was no problem going around the corner, however as soon as they were round Tessa seemed to zigzag all over the place, and all too often when she eventually stopped in a straight line, if Philip asked her to reverse a little more she would start to move in or out. He could feel himself starting to get angry.

'For an intelligent woman you are acting like an idiot,' he shouted. 'Surely you can understand that just because the car is in a straight line, if the front wheels are not straight then as soon as you move again you will move to the right or left depending on which way they are turned.'

'Don't shout at me,' Tessa replied. 'You are supposed to be teaching me, not bullying me. I don't understand why I am going wrong, I think I have done everything you asked me to do, so therefore you obviously have not explained things so I understand.'

Philip decided to call the reverse lesson off for the day and later had a chance to think about what Tessa had said.

The next time they went out and Tessa again experienced the same problem when trying to straighten up Philip said, 'Stop a minute, Tessa, and try going forward slowly round the corner to the position we were in when we first started to reverse.'

Tessa looked surprised; however, she did as she was asked. As soon as she started to turn into the road Philip said, 'Notice how when you are driving forward into this road you are now pulling quite firmly on the steering wheel, now note what you are doing with the wheel once you are round the corner.'

Tessa observed that she started to pull to the right fairly hard, then gave a little pull to the left and right to obtain a nice straight line.

'I see what you mean,' she said. 'I'm sort of feathering the wheel to get a straight course.'

'That's exactly what I am trying to get you to do when you go backwards once round the corner,' said Philip.

After a couple more attempts Tessa was able to do the reverse with reasonable accuracy.

Thomas points out the dangers

Thomas was pleased that his brother Martin had no problems with any of his manoeuvres, but felt he was inclined to carry them out rather fast.

'You're not really checking for other road users enough,' he pointed out. However, it was not until they were practising a reverse park and Martin failed to observe a car coming toward them that the message about observation really was understood.

Martin had just started to turn the wheel to get into the parking place: Thomas noticed the oncoming car at the same moment that its driver gave a very loud hoot which startled Martin, causing him to stall.

'He is a miserable old fellow, no patience and bad mannered,' Martin said angrily as he restarted the engine.

'No,' Thomas retorted. 'It's you who are being impatient, bad mannered and thoughtless.' Martin look surprised. 'Yes,' Thomas said. 'When you are carrying out any manoeuvre you must always look out for other road users and show them consideration. You weren't even aware that the car was coming, as you turned the wheel the front offside end of the car was swinging right out into his path, you could have caused an accident.'

Martin was very subdued, realising the dangers he was causing by rushing everything, which pleased Thomas, who was starting to worry about how safe his brother would be behind a wheel.

DISCUSSION POINTS

1. List five things you should be looking out for when carrying out any manoeuvre.

2. Can you list the advantages of reversing into a parking space as opposed to driving in forward?

3. What are the disadvantages of spending too much time in one period on practising a reverse?

7
Dealing with Hazardous Conditions

Throughout our driving life we encounter many different hazardous conditions: not only fog and snow but even darkness, especially in the rain, are conditions where the driver has to be extra alert and remember to look and plan ahead. It is important that your learner experiences as many different hazardous conditions as is reasonably possible before attempting to take the driving test.

STOPPING IN AN EMERGENCY

During the test the examiner will ask your learner to do an emergency stop: this is one of the skills it is *not* advisable to practise each lesson. Once your pupil can do it, don't practise it again until just before the driving test, as to do it repeatedly is not good for the car, your learner or yourself, and it could cause problems to other road users.

Your pupil's aims will be to:

- stop the car as in an emergency
- control the vehicle
- ensure the wheels don't lock
- use the foot brake correctly
- avoid coasting
- keep two hands on the wheel throughout the whole exercise.

Practising the emergency stop

Before asking your learner to do an emergency stop for practice, do make sure there are no vehicles behind. Emphasise the importance of keeping two hands firmly on the wheel at all times during this exercise, until the car has stopped completely, before applying the hand brake.

If your learner is too quick on the foot brake there is a risk that the wheels will lock causing the vehicle to skid. If this happens ensure that your learner knows how to regain control of the car by immediately lifting the foot off the foot brake and applying it again with a pumping action.

Explain about thinking distances, the distance travelled while thinking what you are going to do. For example, at 30 miles an hour a car travels 9m before even the fastest thinking person can react to an emergency. The car travels another 23m before it stops completely. This is known as braking distance. Therefore the overall stopping distance when travelling at 30mph is 32m. The figures for 50mph are 15m thinking distance, 38m braking distance, making an overall stopping distance of 53m.

If you are using the non metric measure the miles an hour you are travelling is the distance in feet your car will travel while your brain is registering that you are going to stop.

$$40\text{mph} = 40 \text{ ft}$$
$$50\text{mph} = 50 \text{ ft}$$
$$60\text{mph} = 60 \text{ ft.}$$

Remind your learner this is only the thinking distance, to which must be added the braking distance. Full details of overall stopping distances are shown on the back cover of the *Highway Code*.

Remind your learner of the following points:

• The clutch should never be pushed in too early otherwise the car will coast; it should be pushed in at the last moment to allow maximum braking and stability.

• Don't signal: keep both hands on the wheel.

• There is no need to make a special point of looking in the mirror: a driver should know what is behind at all times in any case.

• Look all around before moving off again.

DRIVING IN ALL WEATHERS

Weather conditions can lead to various different hazards, so as far as possible try to take your learner out in different weather conditions on different types of road once they have mastered the art of handling the car in normal conditions.

Driving in the rain
Remind your learner that hazards are doubled in wet conditions,

and perhaps the biggest single danger is being unable to see properly. Remind your learner to:

- put on the wipers to improve vision (often even the most advanced learner drivers don't think to switch on the wipers unless reminded)

- use the demister heater

- use dipped headlights when vision is cut down by heavy rain. Explain that this is not to help our vision but so that we can be seen more easily. Point out how much sooner we can see cars coming towards us with their lights on than those who have forgotten

- keep a good distance from the car in front because stopping distances are at least double when the roads are wet

- pay particular attention to pedestrians, who have a tendency to be more reckless when it's wet: they no doubt feel cold and miserable so they do not take the same care when crossing roads as normal

- adjust speed according to the road and traffic conditions.

Always have a cloth handy to keep the windscreen, windows and mirrors clean. If necessary ask your learner to stop the car to enable you to clean the outside rear window, or any other which has got so wet it is affecting vision.

Particular dangers
Warn your learner of the dangers of:

- **Aquaplaning**, when the water on the road surface causes the car to slide forward on a thin film of water. If this happens explain that the first thing to do is ease off the foot on the accelerator and never use the brake in these conditions.

- **Spray**, when surface water kicked up by other vehicles, particularly lorries, is thrown over the windscreen. This can cause the driver's vision to be lost for a few seconds and is very unnerving.

It is for these reasons that speed must be reduced when driving in the rain.

Driving in high winds

When driving on a very windy day your learner must realise the importance of the correct hold on the steering wheel. The dangers to look out for include:

- cyclists being blown in front of your car: remember to keep a good distance out when passing cyclists
- vehicles, particularly high sided ones, which could be blown off course
- obstacles blowing into the road, so drivers must look well ahead for any debris on the road, and for plastic bags which could blow onto the windscreen and affect vision.

Driving in fog

Fog is one of the most dangerous and frightening weather conditions to drive in. It is advisable not to take your learner out if there is a thick fog: sometimes however, a fog will suddenly come down while you are out on the road so it is always a good idea during a normal lesson to talk about coping with adverse weather conditions. Remind your learner to:

- always keep well away from the vehicle in front in foggy conditions
- never follow the tail light of the vehicle in front in foggy weather, you may end up following it into an accident (multiple pile ups are one of the dangers of driving in fog particularly on motorways)
- drive with dipped headlights on to enable other road users to see you
- keep the windscreen clean at all times
- use the windscreen wipers
- keep nearer the white line than the kerb in thick fog as there may be cyclists or parked cars
- take particular care at traffic lights
- open your window when turning right in thick fog and listen for oncoming vehicles before turning
- drive slowly in foggy conditions.

Remind your learner we should always drive according to our vision.

Driving at night

When you take your learner out in the dark for the first time explain the importance of always ensuring that maximum vision is obtained by:

- cleaning the windows before the journey, and again as necessary during the time you are out
- cleaning the lights, which pick up more dirt than the windscreen.

The learner should also:

- know that oncoming lights can dazzle so the best course of action is to try to keep an eye on your side of the road until the danger is past
- understand when to dip the headlights, and why we need to do it for cyclists as well as cars
- know what to do if the lights of the vehicle behind are causing problems: use the anti-dazzle lever on the interior mirror and slow down if necessary.
- realise how vision ahead is cut down and how difficult it is to see pedestrians, especially in dark clothes, who may be crossing the road
- be prepared for the double danger of driving at night in the rain.

Make sure your learner realises how dangerous it is to break down or run out of petrol at night. Remind them of the importance of checking all lights before making a journey.

Driving in snow and ice

If you are accompanying a learner driver during the winter months you may encounter winter conditions. If you do, remind your learner to:

- increase the distance from the car in front because stopping distances are more than trebled in snow and ice
- keep the rear window clear of snow
- check that the wheel arches are not clogged with snow which would affect the steering and braking
- brake very gently
- anticipate what is happening ahead and change into a lower gear much earlier to avoid braking
- treat every control – brakes, accelerator, steering, clutch and gears

– very delicately, as driving in winter conditions requires the same careful movements as walking on ice or snow
• avoid any sudden movement to help prevent skidding.

Even if you are accompanying your learner driver only in the summer months it is important that at some time you explain about driving in ice and snow.

OVERTAKING

Always ensure that your learner remembers that any change in course when driving requires three important checks, which are:

1. Look in rear view mirrors to ensure that there are no vehicles already on a course to overtake you.

2. Ensure the road ahead is clear.

3. Check that the correct gear is engaged. Remind the learner that slipping into a lower gear is rather like adding an extra horse to a carriage, it gives you extra power when needed.

Always make sure that your learner understands the importance of keeping a good distance from a cyclist and never to overtake a cyclist just before turning left. People learning to drive tend to forget that cyclists have the same rights on the roads as cars.

CHECKLIST

At the end of this session your learner should understand:

• how to do an emergency stop
• how to drive in the rain safely
• the dangers of high winds
• what to do when they encounter fog
• how driving at night requires extra skills
• how to drive in snow and icy conditions
• extra attention is needed when overtaking
• the care and attention needed for cyclists.

QUESTIONS AND ANSWERS

Q *Do I need to indicate when passing a cyclist?*

A The indicator should be used to help other traffic, therefore if there is no vehicle behind you there is no need to indicate. However, if when you check your mirror the vehicle behind is very close or has indicated to overtake you, you must warn them that you are about to change direction by indicating. Early anticipation is best in circumstances like this, so you can take a smooth course to overtake the bicycle; however, in heavy town traffic this is not always possible.

Q *When taking my learner out in rain, particularly when doing the manoeuvres, I find visibility is cut down not only by the inside of the car steaming up, but rain on the outside windows. Is there any way I can prevent this?*

A This is always a problem for any driver in the wet and with a learner, who may be nervous and breathing heavily, it is often particularly acute. Often the dampness is aggravated by the fact that damp clothes, wet shoes and umbrellas are in the vehicle. There is no cure for this dampness in very wet conditions: however, visibility can be improved if you:
- open all the windows a little
- turn the demister towards windscreen and windows
- turn the demister fan on full if it is not too distracting for your learner (many learners find if the fan is turned on they cannot hear the engine and often do not realise that they have stalled)
- keep a cloth in the car for cleaning the inside windows regularly
- stop at regular intervals to clean outside windows with a cloth which you should keep in a plastic bag
- make sure your windscreen washer bottle has plenty of liquid in before starting a session of teaching.

Special products are available which reduce the droplet effect of rain on the windscreen. Use these regularly.

Q *I was involved in an accident once when the car in front stopped suddenly and although I was well behind it my brakes locked and I ended up going into its rear end. What action should I have taken?*

A As soon as you realise your emergency stop is not going to plan, you must lift your foot off the foot brake slightly and apply it again using a pumping action if necessary. It takes a lot of courage sometimes to take your foot off the brake and put it down again – particularly when heading toward a brick wall or another car – however, it is the only way to stop when you are skidding towards danger.

CASE STUDIES

Julie shows how to light up the dark corners

Julie was quite surprised when she first took Susan out in the dark for a drive. At first Susan was very timid and driving far too slowly, but within a very short while she seemed to gain confidence.

'You're really driving well now,' Julie told Susan. 'I am pleased to see you are remembering to dip your headlights whenever a car approaches without being reminded. You could also use your lights on dip for a left hand bend so you can see the left side of the road better and any cyclists and pedestrians who may be on the road. Full beam is best for right hand bends, but not when there is oncoming traffic.'

Julie found this helped Susan's vision on the dark country roads on which they had to drive home.

Philip finds things get steamed up

Philip was just starting to enjoy taking Tessa out for their regular driving practice when they encountered a typical November day, drizzle all the way there, and on the way back patchy fog. Philip had already reminded Tessa to put the headlights on dip, the wipers were going and the warm air from the car heater was turned on the windscreen.

'I can't see properly,' Tessa said. 'The windows either side are all steamed up, and even the front window vision is not good.'

Philip turned the heater fan on full.

'I can't drive with that noise,' said Tessa. 'You will have to take over.'

As Tessa pulled over to stop Philip realised that, although it would be easy for him to drive the rest of the way home, once Tessa had passed her test she was bound to encounter these conditions.

'Let's give it another try,' he said to Tessa. 'Let me clean all the windows inside and out, then we will open all the windows just a fraction to allow air to circulate, and instead of putting the heater fan on full we will try it on half speed to see if it's less distracting for you.'

Although they felt a little cold from the open windows, the vision was improved, enabling Tessa to gain experience of driving in bad weather conditions with safety.

Thomas takes control

Thomas was feeling very confident about Martin's driving so was not worried when it started snowing. It was when he noticed that Martin was gathering speed that the trouble started.

'Hey! watch your speed,' he said. Martin, without thinking, braked. The car immediately went into a skid.

'Take your foot off the brake, turn into the skid,' Thomas commanded. Martin followed his instructions, and was able to correct the skid and get back on course. 'It's easy to become over confident,' Thomas said. 'In driving you always need to keep your concentration on the road and the weather, adjusting your speed accordingly.'

Both Thomas and Martin were shaken by the skid, but felt they had learned a lesson from the incident.

Thomas realised he was wrong to suddenly draw attention to the speed Martin was travelling, especially in such weather conditions. He would have been wiser to have just said, 'ease your foot off the accelerator a little.'

DISCUSSION POINTS

1. List five problems with taking a learner out on a wet day.

2. Do you feel that driving in poor conditions is more tiring?

3. Making a long journey in winter conditions requires extra preparations: how would you prepare for a long journey in these circumstances?

8
Taking the Driving Test

Perhaps more than any other exam or test in life, the driving test causes the most problems with failure often due to the candidate's nerves inhibiting their full potential. The normally timid or nervous person is often able to cope with their nerves on this occasion; it is the confident person who, never having encountered nerves before, sometimes loses concentration and starts to drive badly.

PREPARING FOR THE THEORY TEST

Learners must sit the theory test before they are allowed to sit their practical driving test. You as the person accompanying a learner can help them to pass this test more easily by pointing out the advice and rules in the *Highway Code*, and other aspects of good driving procedure whenever you take your learner out. Always explain *why* we do things and the dangers of not obeying the rules.

Before taking the theory test
Make sure your learner knows and understands:

- the importance of consideration, anticipation and observation
- stopping distances and reaction times
- the effect of drink, drugs, fatigue, ill health and stress on driving
- what constitutes danger to other road users, cyclists, pedestrians, motorcyclists
- the dangers posed by other road users, *eg* lorries, buses
- the effects of different types of road surfaces, road conditions, wind and weather
- the characteristics of different types of road
- road signs and traffic regulations
- the rules on administrative documents used for vehicles
- what to do in the event of an accident
- the safety factors relating to loading the car and towing
- basic mechanics

- use of safety equipment, seat belts *etc*
- how driving affects the environment, fuel consumption, pollution, noise.

By encouraging your learner to read and understand the *Highway Code, The Driving Manual* and the small booklet *The Driving Test*, you will not only help the learner pass the theory test more easily, but also to appreciate the value of good driving practices – which in turn will make it easier to pass the practical driving test and enjoy a lifetime of good driving.

PREPARING FOR THE PRACTICAL TEST

The mock test

It's a good idea to have a mock test with your learner, on roads similar to those which they are going to encounter on the actual test. You might want to have paper and pencil ready to write down the errors your learner makes, and maybe the things done well. Whichever way you do it you will notice that learners drive quite differently when they think they are being tested.

Once you feel your learner is driving reasonably well you need to assess how they drive if you are not there to advise. Do this by just sitting quietly beside, not offering any advice or encouragement.

Your aims
- To simulate test conditions.
- To ensure that your learner is safe to drive alone
  - safely
  - with due consideration to other road users
  - showing knowledge of the rules as set down in the *Highway Code*.
- To observe how your learner acts under the pressure of test conditions.
- To understand how to analyse the faults your learner may make.

Simulating test conditions
Start by checking the learner's eyesight: it's surprising how someone's eyesight can deteriorate in a matter of months, so always check that your learner can read a number plate from a suitable distance away. You could test on the distance between two lamp posts, which is quite a bit more than the 12.2 metres required.

Try to use formal standard expressions as used by the driving examiner, for example:

- 'Please follow the road ahead at all times unless road signs dictate otherwise'
- 'I would like you to take the next available road on the left/right'
- 'Pull up on the left at a convenient place please'.

Have a note pad and pen ready to note down any faults you observe or any points you wish to discuss later. Be prepared for your learner to become very nervous and act out of character.

Common faults to look out for on a mock test

Accelerator	– over acceleration particularly during the manoeuvring exercises
	– fierce use of the clutch
Clutch	– poor coordination of clutch with accelerator
	– pushing the clutch in too early
	– holding the clutch down too long while changing gear
	– resting the foot on clutch pedal slightly while driving
Gears	– allowing the car to coast in neutral
	– rough changing of gears
	– looking down at the gear lever while changing gear
	– not being in the correct gear for the road condition or hazard
	– selecting the incorrect gear and not correcting it immediately
Foot brake	– harsh use of foot brake
Hand brake	– pulling the hand brake on before the vehicle has come to a halt
	– keeping hand on hand brake lever too long when moving off
Steering	– letting the wheel slip through the hands while straightening up
	– crossing the hands while steering
Observation	– lack of forward planning
	– poor anticipation of the actions of other road users
	– not using rear view mirror correctly.

At the end of the mock test, or earlier if you feel your learner is making serious mistakes or one mistake repeatedly, for example indicating too early, pull into a quiet place so you can explain any mistakes and suggest how to rectify them. Always try to give a few words of encouragement as many learners feel they have made so many errors that they will never be ready for the test.

TAKING THE PRACTICAL TEST

The object of the actual driving test is to satisfy the examiner that the candidate can:

- drive safely
- do the set exercises with reasonable accuracy
- show knowledge of the *Highway Code*.

The test will last approximately 35 minutes and will include an eyesight test and special exercises such as:

- emergency stop
- turn in the road
- a reverse round a corner
- a reverse park.

Before the test
Before setting out for the driving test it is a good idea to do a few checks:

- confirm that your learner has a provisional licence and that it is signed
- ensure the car is in good mechanical order
- check there is plenty of petrol in the tank
- examine the car insurance and road fund licence to ensure they are up to date
- make sure the car is clean – this helps give the learner confidence
- ask if your learner has taken any tablets which are not prescribed in the hope that this will help them if they start to feel nervous. This could make their reactions too slow resulting in dangerous driving.

On arrival at the test centre
You can help your learner to feel more relaxed by:

- cleaning all windows again so that your learner will have maximum vision
- knowing where the nearest toilets are and telling your learner
- having some mints handy for your learner to suck to help nerves

- keeping paper tissues ready in the car for the tears of joy or disappointment at the end of the test.

After the test
Make sure you are there waiting when your learner arrives back from the test: regardless of the result they will be in an emotional state and will need you to share their joy at passing, or help them to understand why they did not pass.

UNDERSTANDING THE REASONS FOR FAILURE

If your learner fails the driving test, or as the examiner would say 'has not reached the required standard', the learner will feel a failure and may be very distressed. It's important that you encourage the learner to continue with his driving practice, pointing out that any errors made are far better done during a driving test than when alone in the car. Look carefully at the form that the examiner will have issued; the examiner will have underlined certain items which he or she feels that your learner needs to practise more. This form aims to help the learner improve their driving standards, but unfortunately many people who fail the test are too upset or angry to be able to study the form correctly, therefore your task now is to:

- discuss the 'Statement of Failure' form with your learner
- help your learner understand why the test was failed
- encourage the learner to keep practising their driving
- improve their standard of driving
- note the points the examiner has underlined on the failure form
- explain why the examiner made a note of this point
- learn from the mistakes so that your learner feels more confident and is able to pass the text next time.

Encouraging your learner to try again
Unfortunately after failing a driving test learners are often so despondent that they feel they could never take another test again; it is therefore very important that you encourage your learner to keep going and retake the test. You could point out that:

- learning from mistakes will improve driving skills
- extra lessons will teach extra skills and will prepare them better for the next test
- working harder to achieve anything causes you to value it more,

so a person who fails the driving test initially is more likely to be a better driver than someone who passed the test first time.

Why people fail the driving test

Most people who fail their driving test do so because they make a small error, which most likely would not have caused them to fail, their minds dwell on this causing them to make major mistakes.

Remind your learner:

- never look back at an error
- forget it for the time being and look ahead to the next hazard
- driving is a moving picture which changes all the time, so you need to
  - look ahead
  - plan ahead
  - be alert.

Other errors often made on a driving test are:

- excessive speed caused by nervous tension, trying to get the test over quickly
- driving too slow because the learner is trying to do everything perfectly.

Look carefully at the failure form and notice the exact words underlined: for example, if under the statement:

Make proper use of accelerator, clutch, gears, foot brake, hand brake, steering

only '*Make proper use*' and '*hand brake*' are underlined, then this could mean that your learner is pulling on his hand brake before the car has come to a halt. Watch carefully when your learner is stopping in future to see if this in fact the case. '*Clutch*' underlined could mean that your learner is pushing the clutch in too early when changing gear or when stopping.

The small booklet *The Driving Test* will help with the points underlined on the failure form.

PASSING THE TEST

Passing the driving test is, like falling in love, one of the most exciting and emotional events in life. When most learners pass:

- they can't stop smiling
- they can't stop talking
- they are over excited
- they are unable to drive safely.

After offering your congratulations, remind the learner of his or her responsibilities as a driver. Passing the test is only the start of driving: driving is a skill one always has to try to improve.

Remind the new driver of the dangers of peer pressure when friends may encourage fast driving or overtaking when it's not safe. The new driver should also remember that a car can be a lethal weapon, especially when driven badly. It is a driver's responsibility to drive with care and attention at all times.

Passing the test is only the start of learning to drive: one should aim to improve driving skills, building on the foundation learned so far.

Preparing for a lifetime of safe driving

Suggest to your learner that it is advisable that you come along a couple more times to explain about motorway driving – also, if the learner has only driven in towns, out of town driving requires different skills and encounters more unusual hazards. You could mention that up to this point there have always been two pairs of eyes on the road when you have been out in the car together, and that you have always been there to advise and explain. Good driving requires:

- anticipation
- concentration
- confidence
- patience
- responsibility
- tolerance.

These are the attributes which help to make a good driver.

Most road accidents are caused by driver error: as you hand over the responsibility of handling a car alone, ensure that the new driver is aware of this.

CHECKLIST

At the end of this session you should be able to help your learner to:

- take the theory driving test
- take a mock driving test

- understand what is required from the driving tests
- know their responsibility as a driver if they pass
- know what to do if they fail.

QUESTIONS AND ANSWERS

Q *Do you have to wait a month before you resit a driving test?*

A Up to now a learner who fails a driving test has to wait one calendar month before taking the test again; however, this is now changed and the test can be taken at an earlier time. Do make sure your learner practises to correct any errors listed on the failure form before taking the test again.

Q *Is it true that examiners have to fail a certain percentage of candidates?*

A Each candidate is tested on his or her ability to drive. Examiners would like to pass everybody as it's less paperwork for them. However, many candidates fail to show the examiner good driving procedures, meaning that it could be dangerous to allow them to drive on their own. The examiner only has a short while to decide if the candidate is safe and fit to drive for the rest of their life.

Q *How many hours of tuition do you think a person needs before taking a driving test?*

A A rough guide is 1½ hours for each year of the learner's life. Much depends on the person's attitude and speed in learning new skills – especially the coordination of feet, hands and vision. I taught a young girl in her 20s who needed 60 hours' tuition, on the other hand one of my pupils was a lady in her early 40s who had never sat behind the wheel of a car before and was ready for her test after only 15 hours' driving tuition. As a guide never let anyone sit the driving test until you feel you would be happy for them to drive your family.

CASE STUDIES

Julie tries a different approach
Julie was delighted with the progress which Susan had made and had no worries about putting her in for her driving test. She was therefore greatly surprised when Susan not only failed her test, but the errors listed were skills that she normally had no problem with.

'I'm hopeless,' Susan said as she wiped away the tears of disappointment. 'I will never be able to pass the test – I did everything wrong, even my turn in the road which is one of my best manoeuvres.'

Julie looked at Susan's failure form and noticed that 'Take suitable precautions before starting the engine' was underlined, also 'Make proper use of gears, foot brake, hand brake'.

'Can you remember what happened during the turn in the road?' she asked.

'Everything,' Susan replied tearfully. 'I moved forward to the opposite side of the road, then I stalled the car as I came to a stop. After that it was a complete nightmare; the car jumped forward and hit the kerb when I tried to start it, then stalled again, then after that I can't really remember.'

Julie realised that Susan must have forgotten to put the hand brake on and put the gear lever in neutral before starting the engine, then had panicked which had caused her to rush things and make more errors.

'Let me drive you home now,' Julie said. 'Next time we go out for a drive I will give you a pretend test acting like an examiner, I will not discuss anything with you at all, I will act like a stranger.'

Although initially both Susan and Julie found this approach very difficult, after a while Julie noticed that when Susan made a small error she corrected it automatically and carried on driving well.

Susan passed her test six weeks later.

Philip gets worried
On the day of the test Philip decided to have a final practice so that Tessa would feel confident during her test. He was therefore very worried when Tessa started to have difficultly with her reverse park.

'I can't do it any more,' Tessa said miserably. 'I seem to have lost the knack, I know I am going to fail this test.'

After a couple more attempts, each worse than the previous one, Philip wondered whether he had put Tessa in for the test too early.

'Let me demonstrate one for you,' he suggested.

As he pulled alongside the car he was going to reverse behind and started to reverse he realised that he had started to turn too early. 'I am distracted by worrying about Tessa,' he thought as he pulled forward to start again.

As he parked the car Tessa said, 'That's not allowed, you went forward and started again.'

Philip laughed, 'Well you didn't expect me to carry on and hit the car I was reversing behind, did you?'

'On a test I couldn't do that could I?' Tessa queried.

Philip sounded surprised as he answered, 'I should imagine the examiner would definitely think you were unfit to drive if when you were reversing you carried on even though you realised you were going to hit something.'

'I didn't realise that,' Tessa remarked. 'In that case I have nothing to worry about. I always thought once you had started any reverse you just had to correct it somehow as you were going backwards.'

Tessa took her test, all her manoeuvres were perfect and she passed.

Thomas gets a surprise

Thomas was confident that his brother Martin would sail though his driving test, but was very surprised to notice how nervous he became when they tried a mock test.

'I'm so frightened of failing again,' Martin said. 'As soon as you said let's have a pretend test I started to get worried, all I could think was, what if I failed again, and it is the silence during the test which I remember made matters even worse.'

Thomas tried to think of a way to help his brother relax. 'When you get in the car with the examiner, have a mint, this will help the dry nervous feeling, then when you feel the silence is preying on your nerves, talk to yourself about what you are doing, for example 'I had better keep an eye on that car behind – he is a little too close', or 'The lights have been on red a while so I had better be prepared for them to change as I get there.' The examiner may think you unusual talking to yourself but it may help.'

The following day Thomas tried a mock test with Martin, who followed his brother's advice about sucking a mint and talking to himself. Thomas was pleasantly surprised to find his idea worked.

Martin took his driving test a week later and passed.

DISCUSSION POINTS

1. How do you cope with nerves in an exam and what would you say to a nervous learner before their driving test?

2. Is someone who passes their first test a better driver than someone who fails?

3. Do you think people should take a winter driving test as well as their normal test?

9
Driving on Motorways and Continental Roads

After your learner has passed the test it is advisable that you accompany them for their initial drive on a motorway where not only will traffic be travelling much faster than on normal roads, but a different approach is required when you are entering or exiting a motorway. This will also provide an opportunity to discuss continental driving and the rules and regulations they will encounter when driving in different countries.

Points to remember
- People who have just passed a driving test have no experience of motorway driving.
- Once they have passed the driving test a large proportion of drivers never look at a *Highway Code* again.
- Individuals are very sensitive about their driving and resent criticism.
- Most people think they are good drivers.
- If you are a passenger and you feel nervous about the way the driver is driving, your natural survival instincts are normally correct and your life is being placed in jeopardy by bad driving.
- Instructing someone how to drive is a wonderful opportunity to establish good driving practices and habits in a potential driver.

DRIVING ON THE MOTORWAY

Learner drivers are forbidden on motorways in the UK, so the first chance a person has of getting experience of motorway driving is when they have passed their test. Before going on a motorway for the first time new drivers should:

- be accompanied by an experienced driver
- have a thorough knowledge of the *Highway Code* with reference to motorways.

Before using a motorway

Explain to your new driver the importance of making the following checks before travelling on motorways – if anything goes wrong with the car on the motorway they are placing themselves and their passengers in a very dangerous situation:

- check your tyres
- make sure you have plenty of petrol
- top up your windscreen washer reservoir
- check your oil and water
- clean your windows and lights.

> The most dangerous place on a motorway is on the hard shoulder.

Entering a motorway

It's very important that your new driver understands:

- how to use the slip road to build up a suitable speed to feed into the traffic on the motorway
- why stopping on the slip road, or treating it like a give way on a normal road, could be very dangerous and could cause you to be hit in the rear by the car behind.

Entering a motorway requires new skills, particularly:

- observing the actions of other traffic at a higher speed
- judging when to feed into the fast moving traffic
- adjusting your speed to that of traffic already on the motorway.

Driving on the motorway

Once on the motorway you will have an opportunity to point out to your new driver the various markings and signs and explain their meanings. Also impress on them the importance of:

- using rear view and side mirrors more often as traffic is travelling so much faster and they need to have a clear all round vision of what is happening in all lanes
- understanding lane discipline: always driving in the nearside lane unless overtaking, the third lane is for overtaking two lanes of vehicles

- looking as far ahead as possible
- anticipating the actions of other vehicles at all times
- being alert to all dangers
- knowing the meaning of the danger signals on the motorway and how to react to them
- tolerating the bad habits and manners of other drivers who may be tired or under pressure to reach a certain destination.

Leaving a motorway

Advise your new driver that when you need to leave the motorway you do not slow down on the actual motorway, you use the slip roads. Slip roads are:

- marked by green studs on the edge of the road
- best entered on their left-hand lane
- used for deceleration, slowing down to adjust to the new road ahead.

When in the slip road:

- check your speedometer – you are very likely travelling a lot faster than you thought
- remember 30 miles an hour can seem very slow after travelling at speeds up to 70.

Dangers on the motorway

Because of the high speeds encountered on motorways your new driver should be aware of the dangers when driving at speed. The biggest problems are:

1. fog
2. spray from heavy vehicles in wet conditions
3. tiredness often brought on by boredom.

Advise your new driver that, when driving at speed, to reduce the risk of accident by:

- keeping plenty of space between themselves and the vehicle in front: this helps reduce the risk of motorway pile ups
- checking all mirrors before changing lanes
- anticipating problems ahead before they develop into a dangerous situation

- looking quickly to the side before changing lanes to counteract blind spots
- paying attention to the overhead signs
- moving into the correct lane in good time at motorway interchanges.

DRIVING ON THE CONTINENT

At some time your new driver may want to drive on the Continent or further afield. It is a good idea to explain about the different types of signs and traffic conditions they are going to encounter.

Most drivers worry about driving on the right, but a bigger hazard for British drivers is understanding the rule of the right.

The rule of the right
- In many Continental countries a yellow diamond sign denotes that vehicles travelling on that road have priority over vehicles entering the road from the right.
- Where there is a yellow diamond with a black line through it you must give way to any traffic entering your road from the right.
- On town and country roads where there are no signs you always give way to vehicles entering from the right.

Roundabouts
On approaching roundabouts check if you have a give way or priority on approach. On some roundabouts you have to give way to vehicles entering the roundabout.

Speed
The speed in some countries is higher than in Britain, particularly in Germany where there is only a recommended maximum speed on motorways, so many vehicles are travelling in excess of 100mph.

- Remember to be extra watchful when entering a motorway.
- Use your indicator whenever you intend to change lanes and again when you return to your own lane.
- Look as far ahead as you can and plan your actions accordingly.
- Know your route and road numbers and have them displayed where you can see them at a glance.

CHECKLIST

At the end of this session your new driver should understand:

- the importance of checking the car before driving on a motorway
- how to enter and leave a motorway
- the importance of extra observation
- the dangers of motorway driving
- a little about Continental driving
- the rule of the right as practised on the Continent.

QUESTIONS AND ANSWERS

Q *If I am travelling at 70mph on the motorway, the maximum speed allowed in the UK, is it advisable to keep to the middle lane?*

A When travelling in the middle you have effectively reduced a three lane motorway to a two lane one which can cause drivers to take chances by 'undertaking' you on the inside – a recipe for disaster. Keep to the inside lane except when overtaking.

Q *I understand that in certain countries driving lessons include driving on motorways and on the driving test candidates have to drive on normal roads and motorways. Is this true?*

A In Germany learner drivers are taught on both normal roads and the autobahn; however, this is a country which is crisscrossed with motorways (autobahns) and before driving on any road the German learner driver has to attend many hours of classroom tuition on the rules and regulations for drivers. In addition only a professional driving instructor can accompany a learner driver – it is forbidden by law for a lay person to take a driver out for practice.

Q *We live in the very north of Scotland where the nearest motorway is over 200 miles away, and although I have been driving for four years I have never been on a motorway so I feel I am not in a position to advise my new driver on this matter. What would you suggest?*

A Even people who have had motorway experience have to re-educate themselves if they are not using motorways regularly. Remember after four years you no doubt have good handling experience of your car and feel confident driving it, therefore I would advise you and your new driver to refer to the motorway section in *The Driving Manual,* which is the reference book for every driver, before taking a journey that involves going on the motorway.

CASE STUDIES

Julie gets a fright
Julie felt a bit apprehensive about accompanying Susan on the motorway for the first time, as although Susan was handling the car well, the motorway near where they lived was very busy, especially at tea time which was the only time that both Susan and Julie were available. However, the entrance on to the busy motorway went without a hitch and Julie started to relax as Susan handled the car and the traffic well.

'We will leave by the next exit,' Julie suggested as Susan overtook a line of slow moving traffic.

Susan suddenly started to brake causing Julie to shout a warning: 'Don't brake, we are a long way from the exit and that is so dangerous!' She could feel herself shaking with fright at how near the vehicle behind had come to going into their rear end. Susan replied nervously, 'I'm sorry, but I thought I had better slow down and get into this lane of traffic on the inside so that I was ready for the exit.'

Julie realised she should have sat down with Susan and explained more about the rules and regulations of motorway driving, which she subsequently did before they went on the motorway again.

Philip feels proud of Tessa
Soon after Tessa passed her driving test Philip decided they should have a holiday in Bavaria. 'Although it's a long drive through Germany,' he said, 'with two drivers it should prove no problem.'

They had both felt pleased at the way they were handling the traffic on the motorway in Holland and were feeling relaxed as they entered the German autobahn near Venlo. After about an hour they decided it was time to stop for a meal and to change drivers, as Tessa had been driving for a while. Philip was looking at the map when he realised that Tessa had cancelled her right indicator, which she had put on to inform drivers behind that she intended to leave the autobahn, and was already passing the exit lane.

'I thought we were going to stop there,' he said.

'Look back,' Tessa replied. 'There has just been an accident on the run in to that service station: a car decided to overtake the vehicle in front of me then turned into the slip road. I just checked my mirror, altered my indicator and carried on. I thought it better to stop at the next place.'

Philip felt very proud of Tessa's reaction to the accident and congratulated her on her quick thinking.

Thomas finds things get steamed up

Thomas and Martin were travelling to the north of England when they ran into heavy rain; the spray from the lorries was causing visibility problems, the windscreen washers and wipers were on non stop, and the car interior was getting steamed up as quickly as Thomas tried to clean it. They had tried opening the windows a little but the rain was getting them both very wet.

'This is getting a little dangerous,' Thomas remarked, 'also I think our windscreen washer liquid must be getting very low. There is no service station on this motorway for a while but I notice there's an exit shortly: let's leave the motorway and find a garage so we can top up the petrol and check our oil, water, tyres and windscreen water. We could also enquire about something we can wipe the inside of the windows with to stop them misting up.'

They found a garage which provided them with all their needs and could furnish them with a quick meal and a cup of coffee. When they were ready to carry on their journey they not only found their vision better but they both felt refreshed and more alert after their short break.

DISCUSSION POINTS

1. Should learner drivers be able to have lessons on the motorway and motorway driving be part of the driving test?

2. Road rage is getting more common: how do you cope with other people's driving?

3. Leaving a motorway can be very dangerous for many reasons: how many can you think of?

10
Explaining Advanced
Driving Techniques

LOOKING AT DEFENSIVE DRIVING

Most accidents are caused by a mistake on the part of the driver, few can be attributed to any particular road feature or fault with the vehicle. Aggression, intolerance, impatience, selfishness and exhibitionism cause accidents; we all make mistakes at times and should be prepared to make allowances for the mistakes of others.

Always be critical of your own driving; the perfect driver does not exist, so whatever stage you may have reached as a driver, aim for a higher standard. Watch other drivers, copy the best of what you see and learn from their mistakes.

Driving skills alone will not prevent you getting involved in an accident. Developing the right attitude and behaviour is something you should always be working at.

Aims of a good driver
- Show courtesy and consideration at all times.
- Anticipate actions of other road users and changes in road or weather conditions, and hazards at all times.
- Concentrate on your driving and be aware of what is happening on all four sides of your vehicle.
- Have a sense of responsibility.
- Be patient.
- Handle your vehicle with confidence.

It's always worth remembering that you are in charge of the car, not the car in charge of you, so always ensure that you keep it under control.

Avoiding the vehicle in front
Many minor accidents happen when a vehicle goes into the car in front; this type of accident does not often result in serious personal

injury unless high speeds are involved, but it can cause extensive body damage to both vehicles.

The dangers
- ignorance of stopping distances
- poor condition of road surface
- bad weather conditions
- poor visibility – dazzling sunlight – dusk – fog – rain
- slow reaction times
- defective brake lights on the vehicle in front
- vehicle ahead rolling backwards
- an accident pile up
- a vehicle without lights parked on the side of the road at night
- a hazard around the bend – road works – parked vehicle – accident
- driving too close to the vehicle in front
- failing to apply the hand brake correctly when the car is stopped, usually on a slope at lights or road junctions
- failing to anticipate the actions of the vehicle in front.

The defensive tactics
1. Knowing and remembering your stopping distances and keeping your distance from the vehicle in front – if a car comes between you be tolerant and drop back a little.

2. Looking well ahead at all times.

3. Applying the hand brake correctly when stationary – at lights or road junction do keep an eye on the vehicle in front and check that you are not gently rolling forward or the car in front is rolling back.

4. Remembering that most roads have cambers and even a small slope can cause a vehicle to roll slowly forward or backwards.

5. Keeping a safe waiting distance between you and the car in front when stationary – a good guide is to be able to see the bottom of the tyres of the car in front, if you can't you are too close.

6. Anticipating the actions of not only the vehicle directly in front of you but other road users ahead, so you can see a hazard well in advance. For example: you notice a vehicle three or four ahead

of you is showing stop lights; be prepared to slow down even before the vehicle directly ahead does so.

7. Making sure your vehicle is always checked regularly.

8. Being in the right gear for the situation at all times.

Avoiding the vehicle behind

Quite often you can avoid being involved in an accident caused by an inattentive driver by being alert to what is happening all around you; even the smallest bump can cause delays and minor injuries like whiplash or bruising. Also the cost and time taken for repairs to a vehicle can cause worry and frustration.

The dangers
- following driver is too close
- following driver is not paying attention
- following driver is going too fast
- positioning your vehicle too late
- stalling your vehicle – false start
- changing your mind suddenly
- failing to apply the hand brake when your vehicle is stationary so your car rolls back
- failing to check that your lights or brake lights are in good working order so traffic behind is unaware of your intentions
- failing to anticipate
- forgetting to use the mirrors correctly.

The defensive tactics
1. Slow down carefully if driver behind is too close.

2. If you notice the driver behind is not paying attention and you are about to stop at, for example, traffic lights, you should take your foot off the foot brake and apply it again a couple of times; your stop lights will flash and hopefully attract the attention of the driver behind.

3. Plan well ahead so you can check your mirror, signal, then take the necessary course; try to avoid any sudden movements with your controls.

Always try to include all these points in driving practice with your learner – remember the more information on road safety you are able to impart to a learner, the better driver they will be.

LOOKING AT ADVANCED OBSERVATION TECHNIQUES

Looking and planning ahead is perhaps the most difficult part of learning to drive. In the early stages of learning a new learner has to concentrate so hard on the basics of coordinating clutch, accelerator, brakes, gears and steering that they find it difficult to have all round vision. Once their coordination of hands and feet is smooth try to build up their field of vision by taking them on a variety of different roads.

Your pupil's aims will be to:

- understand the importance of forward planning when driving
- anticipate possible dangers in good time
- predict the dangers of unauthorised signals
- know what is happening on all sides of the vehicle at all times
- avoid involvement in accidents
- be in the right gear at the right time in the right position in the road
- increase the field of vision.

To help your student to achieve these aims you will need to know what **you** should be looking for. Initially it's a good idea to explain as much as possible with small sketches and examples.

Unauthorised signals

It is important for your pupil to understand why it is dangerous to wave or indicate in any way that a pedestrian or another vehicle should proceed. As a driver you cannot speak or indicate for the rest of the road users around you, so while you may be willing to wait for another driver, a cyclist or car could be passing on your inside and indirectly you would be partly responsible if the turning car hit the cyclist or car. Another example of unauthorised signalling is when you indicate to a pedestrian that you will wait for them to cross the road, while perhaps unaware that another driver is about to overtake you maybe presuming that you have a problem.

Emphasise that your pupil must remember if another driver waves him on:

– think
– check carefully for other vehicles.

Dangers of parked vehicles

Many roads are now lined with parked vehicles which can cause many problems. The three main dangers are:

1. Difficulty of seeing past parked cars when trying to pull into another road. The answers is to move forward gently until the front of your vehicle is on a line with the outside of the vehicle obstructing your view – cars on the road you are entering will be taking a course to overtake this car – then inch forward very slowly until you can see clearly.

2. Cars parked too near a pedestrian crossing can obstruct the view of people who may have started to cross the road. Always drive with extra care and observation when approaching a pedestrian crossing.

3. In a line of parked cars there is always a risk of cars pulling out, prams or wheelchairs being pushed out into the road, children or car doors opening. Always be extra observant when passing parked cars; try to get an early view of a potential danger by looking ahead under the cars for a view of feet.

Dangers of obstructed view

If your view is obstructed by a tree, house, wall or even a person, the same advice applies as with parked cars: move forward slowly and carefully. It's no good saying a prayer and hoping that all will be clear – just gently and slowly move forward, using clutch control until your field of vision is clear.

CHECKLIST

At the end of this session your pupil should understand:

- how to avoid hitting or being hit by another vehicle
- the importance of looking and planning ahead in driving
- the dangers of unauthorised signals.

QUESTIONS AND ANSWERS

Q *When stopped at lights must I always apply my hand brake?*

A It is always advisable to apply the hand brake and put the gear lever into neutral when stopping at traffic lights or queuing behind other vehicles, unless the wait is likely to be very short.

Q *I have the occasional use of my mother's car but am concerned that I am not getting practice in reading the road and anticipation. Have you any ideas how I can get more practice?*

A You don't have to be driving to practise reading the road: you can do it when you are a passenger in a car or bus, even when you are riding a bicycle.

Q *If I am blinded by oncoming lights what should I do?*

A Slow down, even stop if necessary; don't look directly at the lights, look more towards the kerb. Do not flash your lights.

DISCUSSION POINTS

1. Many people are now concerned with the effect of pollution from motor vehicles; do you think people should be restricted to driving so many miles a week?

2. Driving is a skill which if taught well can enable someone to enjoy many years of safe driving; do you therefore think that it should part of the curriculum in the top forms in schools?

3. Many people like to smoke when they are driving; can you think of five points which you could put to a smoker to discourage them?

Sample Test Questions

The theory test for drivers was introduced in Great Britain in 1996. Here are 35 typical questions to stimulate the mind. Candidates are given 40 minutes to answer all 35 questions. To pass the test they must have 30 correct. Stress to your pupil that the more they study the *Highway Code*, also the two books written by the Driving Standards Agency, *The Driving Test* and *The Driving Manual*, the better the chances of passing the theory test and also the practical driving test.

1. Which is correct (*select one answer*)
   To help drivers on the motorways at night, there are red, green and amber coloured studs. Where would you see the amber studs?

   □ dividing the lanes near interchanges
   □ the left hand edge of the road
   □ the right hand edge of the road
   □ the centre of the road.

2. According to the *Highway Code* which is correct (*select one answer*)
   On a motorway

   □ you must only overtake on the right
   □ you can overtake on any side if it's safe to do so
   □ you may use the lane to the right of a stream of slower vehicles to overtake them but return to the lane to your left when you have passed them.

3. When approaching a roundabout on a dual carriageway and you want to take the third exit should you on entering the roundabout (*select two answers*)

   □ be indicating right
   □ indicating left

□ have no indicator showing
□ be in the right lane on approach
□ be in the left lane on approach.

4. When overtaking motorcyclists, pedal cyclists or horse riders
does the *Highway Code* advise (*select one answer*)

□ you allow half a car's width
□ you allow 1 metre
□ give them as much room as you would a car
□ cross the centre of the road.

5. Which is correct (*select one answer*)
You can supervise a learner driver

□ once you have passed your own driving test
□ if you have held a full British driving licence for one year
□ if you have held a full British driving licence for two years
□ if you are at least 21 and have held a full British driving
licence for that type of car for at least three years.

6. Which is correct (*select two answers*)
When parking at night

□ you must not park facing against a flow of traffic
□ you must be at least 8 metres away from any junction
□ you must be at least 10 metres away from any junction
□ you must always have side lights on when parking in towns.

7. Which of the following information is not found in the *Highway
Code* (*select one answer*)

□ advice on vehicle security
□ advice on first aid
□ advice on Continental driving
□ information on penalty points.

8. At traffic lights the red light is follows by (*select one answer*)

□ red and amber together
□ amber
□ green
□ amber and green together.

9. The hard shoulder of a motorway can be used for which of the
    following (*select one answer*)

    □ joining the motorway
    □ overtaking
    □ stopping to rest when feeling tired
    □ stopping only in an emergency.

10. If travelling along a motorway and your luggage falls off the roof
    rack, should you (*select one answer*)

    □ pull immediately onto the hard shoulder and try to retrieve it
    □ put your four way flashers on and stop in the lane you are in
    □ keep driving and stop at the next emergency phone to inform
      motorway police
    □ do an emergency stop.

11. What is the maximum speed limit for cars and motorcycles on a
    single carriageway, not in a built up area (*select one answer*)

    □ 30mph
    □ 40mph
    □ 50mph
    □ 60mph
    □ 70mph.

12. Signs which are circular and have a red circle around the edge are
    (*select two answers*)

    □ mostly prohibitive
    □ signs giving orders
    □ mainly directional signs
    □ found on motorways.

13. When learning to drive it is advisable to practise your driving
    (*select one answer*)

    □ mainly on test routes
    □ only in daylight
    □ mainly on country road
    □ on as many different types of road as you can.

14. The eyesight test to drive a car or motorcycle requires you to be able to read a vehicle number plate with letters 79.4mm (3.1 inches) high at a distance of (*select one answer*)

   □ 20.5 metres
   □ 20 metres
   □ 19.5 metres
   □ 19 metres.

15. If you cannot read the number on the eyesight test the examiner will (*select one answer*)

   □ fail you immediately
   □ cancel the test until you have your eyes tested by an optician
   □ measure the exact distance and repeat the test
   □ advise you to take two paces forward and try again.

16. If you stall the car what must you do (*select two answers*)

   □ depress the clutch and start the engine again
   □ apply the hand brake
   □ put gear in neutral before starting the engine
   □ put on the four way flashers.

17. In a box junction (*select one answer*)

   □ you are never allowed to stop
   □ you can wait in the box if you are wanting to turn right and are prevented from doing so by oncoming traffic
   □ it is permitted to stop in the box if at traffic lights and your light is green
   □ box junctions are only placed at traffic lights.

18. What should you do when approaching a double unbroken line across the carriageway at the end of a road (*select one answer*)

   □ you must stop even if you can see clearly on approach that the road you are entering is clear
   □ be prepared to stop at the white lines; however, if the road ahead is clear you may proceed with caution without stopping completely
   □ the lines are guide lines to inform you that you are coming to

the end of a road, so proceed as for a give way
- □ providing you are in low gear there is no need to stop.

19. When leaving your car parked facing uphill on the left hand side of the road, is it advisable to (*select one answer*)

- □ pull your steering wheel to the right so your front wheels are turned to the right
- □ pull your steering wheel to the left so that your front wheels are turned to the left
- □ make sure your steering wheel is in the centre position so your front wheels are facing straight ahead
- □ park at an angle with the car front facing the kerb slightly.

20. It is not advisable to mix radial and crossply tyres. However, if you can't avoid mixing types then which is correct (*select one answer*)

- □ any mix is suitable if you have a four-wheel-drive vehicle
- □ radials must always be on the back
- □ radials must always be on the front
- □ if you have to use the spare which is the different type, you must use it on the front near side.

21. If you need to turn right in thick fog should you (*select two answers*)

- □ turn as quickly as possible without hesitation
- □ sound your horn and wait with your foot brake on and listen for other drivers before turning
- □ stop the car, get out and check before turning
- □ turn your radio off and open your window.

22. When driving through a flood should you (*select one answer*)

- □ select first gear, keep the engine speed high and slip the clutch
- □ drive through in second gear keeping the engine speed low
- □ drive through as fast as you can in third gear, which will give you extra acceleration
- □ to avoid stalling keep in fourth gear, with revs high.

23. Which of the following is **not** true (select one answer)

  ☐ you must not drive your vehicle if the car horn is not in working order
  ☐ you must not drive your vehicle if the speedometer is not working
  ☐ you must not drive your vehicle if the stop lights are not working
  ☐ you must not drive your vehicle if the petrol gauge is faulty.

24. On a single track road, if you see a vehicle coming and the passing place is in front of you on the right, do you (*select one answer*)

  ☐ stop immediately and wait for the oncoming car to reach the passing place
  ☐ reverse back to the last passing place on the left
  ☐ drive into the passing place on the right and wait for the oncoming car to pass
  ☐ move forward and wait opposite the passing place on your right.

25. According to the *Highway Code* you must not use your horn at certain times (*select two answers*)

  ☐ between 11.00 pm and 7.00 am in a built up area
  ☐ between 11.30 pm and 7.00 am in a built up area
  ☐ between 12 midnight and 6.00 am in a built up area
  ☐ when your vehicle is stationary, unless a moving vehicle poses a danger
  ☐ when you are near a hospital and have passed the appropriate sign stating so.

26. When driving past animals, which according to the *Highway Code* is correct (*select one answer*)

  ☐ you must sound your horn in plenty of time to warn of your presence
  ☐ you must slow down and stop if necessary
  ☐ you must pass them as quickly and safely as possible
  ☐ treat them as you would a bicycle or slow moving vehicle, overtaking by keeping well to the right.

27. In the *Highway Code* you are advised to watch out for blind and partially signed people who may be carrying white sticks. You are also advised to look out for people who are deaf and blind: which of the following denotes a person who suffers from the double affliction (*select one answer*)

☐ they will carry a white stick with a black band half way down
☐ they will carry a white stick with a reflective yellow band
☐ they will carry a white stick with a red reflective band
☐ they will carry a white stick with two red reflective bands.

28. If your car breaks down on a railway crossing which of the following should you do first (*select one answer*)

☐ get everyone out of the vehicle and clear of the crossing
☐ use the railway telephone immediately to tell the signal operator and follow the instructions given
☐ push the vehicle off the crossing
☐ sound your horn loudly to attract attention.

29. According to the *Highway Code* traffic signs which are triangular are mostly (*select one answer*)

☐ prohibitive
☐ compulsory
☐ warning signs
☐ signs marking primary routes.

30. When changing a wheel which of the following is correct (*select one answer*)

☐ chock up the wheel to be changed before you start
☐ slightly loosen the wheel nuts before you jack up the car
☐ tighten the wheel nuts fully before you lower the jack
☐ release the hand brake if you are changing a rear wheel.

31. When driving round a right hand bend which of the following statements is correct (*select one answer*)
☐ your right hand wheels turn faster
☐ your left hand wheels turn faster
☐ all wheels turn at the same speed
☐ the front wheels always turn faster than the rear wheels.

32. Which of the following is **not** true (*select one answer*)
Tyre wear can be caused by

☐ a fault in the suspension of the car
☐ a fault in the braking system
☐ the timing needs adjustment
☐ poor coordination of clutch and accelerator by driver.

33. Flashing one's headlights is often used in driving. Which according to the *Highway Code* is their correct use (*select one answer*)

☐ to let other road users know you are going to carry on
☐ to let other road users known you are willing to wait
☐ to inform other road users that they have forgotten to dip their lights
☐ to let other road users know that you are there.

34. When approaching lights and they turn to green, do you understand it to mean that (*select one answer*)

☐ it's safe to proceed
☐ slow down and check if it's safe to proceed
☐ you may drive on if the way is clear
☐ put your foot well down on the accelerator to clear the junction as quickly as possible.

35. A continuous line in the centre of the road with a dotted line alongside it on your side means (*select one answer*)

☐ you can overtake but oncoming vehicles cannot
☐ you cannot overtake but oncoming vehicles can
☐ no overtaking by anyone
☐ anyone may overtake but extra caution is required.

Notes and Answers to Sample Test Questions

When teaching someone to drive use every opportunity to point out the various road signs and try to explain the various rules and the reason for a code of behaviour. The sample test questions could be used:

- As a basis for study after the lesson: for example, if you gave question 1 to be answered before the start of the next lesson, in searching for the answer your learner would also discover the answer to three more possible questions – the position of red, green and white studs.

- As a discussion point, in the car, over a cup of coffee, or with a group: for example, question 19 could cause some interesting discussions, as could question 21.

- As a preparation for the next lesson: for example, question 3 would be an ideal question for your learner to study before you have a lesson on roundabouts.

- To revise an earlier lesson: for example, question 16.

- To help your learner pass the theory driving test.

ANSWERS

1. Right hand edge of the road.
2. You may use the lane to the right to overtake slower vehicles but return to the lane to your left when you have passed them.
3. Be indicating right.
   Be in the right lane on approach.
4. Give them as much room as you would a car.
5. If you are at least 21 and have held a full British driving licence

for that type of car for at least three years.

6. You must not park facing against the flow of traffic.
   You must be at least 10 metres away from any junction.
7. Advice on Continental driving.
8. Red and amber together.
9. Stopping only in an emergency.
10. Keep driving and stop at the next emergency phone to inform the police.
11. 60mph.
12. Mostly prohibitive.
    Signs giving orders.
13. On as many different types of road as you can.
14. 20.5 metres.
15. The examiner will measure the exact distance and repeat the test.
16. Apply the hand brake.
    Put gear in neutral before starting the engine.
17. You can wait in the box if you are wanting to turn right and are prevented from doing so by oncoming traffic.
18. You must stop even if you can see clearly on approach that the road you are entering is clear.
19. Pull your steering wheel to the right so that your front wheels are turned to the right.
20. Radials must always be on the back.
21. Sound your horn and wait with your foot brake on and listen for other drivers before turning.
    Turn your radio off and open your window.
22. Select first gear, keep the engine speed high and slip the clutch.
23. You must not drive your vehicle if the petrol gauge is faulty.
24. Move forward and wait opposite the passing place on your right.
25. Between 11.30 pm and 7.00 am in a built up area.
    When your vehicle is stationary, unless a moving vehicle poses a danger.
26. You must slow down and stop if necessary.
27. They will carry a white stick with two red reflective bands.
28. Get everyone out of the vehicle and clear of the crossing.
29. Warning signs.
30. Slightly loosen the wheel nuts before you jack up the car.
31. Your left hand wheels turn faster.
32. The timing needs adjustment.
33. To let other road users know you are there.
34. You may drive on if the way is clear.
35. You can overtake but oncoming vehicles cannot.

Glossary

Advanced motorist. A driver who has improved his standard of driving and has taken a further driving test with the Institute of Advanced Motorists.

Aquaplaning. In wet weather when your vehicle loses its grip on the road surface and starts to slide on a thin film of water.

Biting point. The point when the clutch plates are engaged. You must be able to recognise it when you lift up the clutch pedal.

Blind spot. When a solid object, bodywork of a car, a pedestrian or a tree, interferes with vision often hiding a potential danger. The most common blind spot is when a vehicle behind is not in your rear view mirror as he is at the point of overtaking you.

Block change. Changing from one gear to another without using an intermediate gear: for example, changing from fourth gear to second gear without using third gear.

Box junction. A junction marked by crisscross yellow lines on the road.

Braking distance. The distance the car will travel after you have applied the brakes.

Chevron. Area of diagonal white stripes painted on the road to separate traffic lanes or to protect traffic turning right.

Classified road. Type of road, from motorway to A or B road. Unclassified roads are normally country lanes.

Coasting. When the vehicle is moving but not driven by the engine, caused by either the clutch pedal being held down or the gear being in neutral. This is an illegal practice.

Defensive driving. Planned driving by observation and anticipating what might happen before it actually does.

Driving Standards Agency. The agency of the Department of Transport which conducts all driving tests and is the authoritative body for all matters relating to driving techniques.

Dual controls. An extra clutch and foot brake fitted to a car used for teaching learner drivers.

Emergency stop. A sudden unplanned stop such as when a child runs into the road in front of your vehicle.

Endorsement. A record of a motoring offence on a driving licence.

Full driving licence. The licence given once you have passed the driving tests.

Hazard, road. Any situation which could involve a change of speed or course.

Legal requirement. Knowledge of penalties which can be imposed for road traffic offences as laid out in the *Highway Code*.

MSM. Mirror, Signal, Manoeuvre: the correct sequence before carrying out any driving movement.

Night vision. Limited vision caused through darkness and reflection of lights.

Non classified road. Road without markings.

Overall stopping distance. The braking distance added to the thinking distance (the distance which you travel before your brain reacts to the situation and informs your foot to start braking).

Penalty points. Points given for driving offences which if accumulated to 12 or more over a three year period result in being disqualified from driving for a set period.

Position – speed – look. PSL: check your vehicle is in the correct position, travelling at the correct speed, and looking and acting on what you see.

Provisional driving licence. A licence which allows a learner to drive when accompanied by a suitable experienced driver.

Statement of failure form. A form given to a person who fails their driving test giving details of the mistakes made on the test, and where more practice is required.

Theory test. A written test to be passed before you can take the practical test.

Useful Addresses

Automobile Association, Fanum House, Basingstoke, Hants RG21 2EA.

Department of Transport, Driver and Vehicle Licensing Centre, Swansea SA99 1AN.

Disabled Drivers' Assessment Centre, Banstead Mobility Centre, Park Road, Banstead, Surrey SM7 3EE.

British Institute of Traffic Education and Research, Kent House, Kent Street, Birmingham BF5 6OF.

Driving Instructors Association, Lion Green Road, Coulsdon, Surrey CR3 2NL.

Driving Standards Agency, Stanley House, Talbot Street, Nottingham NG1 5GU.

Guild of Experienced Motorists, Station Road, Forest Row, East Sussex RH18 5EN.

HMSO Bookshop, 40 High Holborn, London WC1V 6HB.

Institute of Advanced Motorists, Empire House, Chiswick High Road, London W4 5TJ.

Motor Schools Association Ltd, 182A Heaton Moor Road, Stockport, Cheshire SK4 4DU.

National Association of Approved Driving Instructors, 90 Ash Lane, Hale Barns, Altrincham, Cheshire WA15 8PB.

Royal Automobile Club, RAC House, Lansdowne Road, Croydon, Surrey CR9 2JA.

Royal Society for the Prevention of Accidents, Cannon House, The Priory, Queensway, Birmingham.

Further Reading

The Driving Manual, Driving Standards Agency (HMSO).
The Driving Instructor's Handbook, John Miller and Nigel Stacey (Kogan Page Ltd).
Help Yourself to Pass the Test, A Holyland (A Holyland).
Pass the Test First Time, Gordon Cole (Ian Allen Ltd).
The Driving Test, Driving Standards Agency (HMSO).
The Highway Code, Driving Standards Agency (HMSO).

Index

MAKING A COMPLAINT
How to put your case successfully and win redress

Helen Shay

Whether you've bought faulty shoes or been sold an unsuitable investment; been over-charged by a bank or suffered the holiday from hell, this book guides you through the maze of complaints procedures, courts, ombudsmen and other forms of consumer redress. It makes the law user-friendly and shows you how to obtain compensation – fast. It shows the way to cut through the aggravation and achieve the best solution for you. Helen Shay is a solicitor of twelve years' standing. She has worked both in private practice and as an in-house lawyer for a major high street retailer – so has experience of consumer disputes from both sides. Currently with an ombudsman's office, she is well-versed in current consumer issues and the problems which can confront the individual versus large organisations. She also tutors and lectures part-time in commercial law, and is knowledgeable in contract, consumer credit, banking law, conveyancing and other legal areas affecting everyday life.

128pp. illus. 1 85703 102 4.

HELPING YOUR CHILD TO READ
How to prepare the child of today for the world of tomorrow

Jonathan Myers

Would you like your child to be able to read well? How do you support your child's reading – at school and at home? Who do you ask for advice? What games and activities are useful? What should you look for when buying books? When does a reading problem need expert attention? How do you check your child's progress? In our fast moving, computerised world, reading is absolutely vital. It is the key basic skill that children and adults need to transmit information. And reading is fun too. With its lively text, examples and case studies, this forward looking book shows how easy it is for you to get your child on the right road to reading success. Jonathan Myers BSc PGCE is an educational consultant and teacher specialising in reading development, dyslexia and a wide range of associated problems.

141pp. illus. 1 85703 192 X.

MANAGING YOUR PERSONAL FINANCES
How to achieve financial security and survive the shrinking welfare state

John Claxton

Life for most people has become increasingly beset by financial worries, and meanwhile the once-dependable prop of state help is shrinking. Today's financial world is a veritable jungle full of predators after your money. This book will help you to check your financial health and prepare a strategy towards creating your own welfare state and financial independence. Find out in simple language with many examples and case studies how to avoid debt, how to finance your home, how to prepare for possible incapacity or redundancy and how to finance your retirement, including care in old age. Discover how to acquire new financial skills, increase your income, reduce outgoings, and prepare to survive in a more self-reliant world. John Claxton is a chartered management accountant and chartered secretary; he teaches personal money management in adult education.

160pp. illus. 1 85703 328 0.

WINNING CONSUMER COMPETITIONS
How to scoop valuable cash and other prizes time and time again

Kathy Kantypowicz

The definitive guide to winning competitions, this volume will show you how you too can stake your claim to some of the millions of glittering prizes offered to consumers every year. Learn how to find entry forms, research your answers and, most important of all, write those few well chosen tie-breaker words which can scoop cars, family holidays, household appliances, clothing, TV and hi-fi equipment, cash and almost any other luxury item you care to name. Why buy when you can win? This book may revolutionize your shopping habits forever. It's easy and it's fun to be a winner! Kathy Kantypowicz has won more than £200,000 worth of prizes and is dubbed 'The Queen of Competitions' by the British press. Now editor of *Competitors World* magazine, she was formerly resident competition expert on *The Big Breakfast Show* and has appeared regularly in television, press and radio features.

116pp. illus. 1 85703 333 7.

How To Books

How To Books provide practical help on a large range of topics. They are available through all good bookshops or can be ordered direct from the distributors. Just tick the titles you want and complete the form on the following page.

- Apply to an Industrial Tribunal (£7.99)
- Applying for a Job (£7.99)
- Applying for a United States Visa (£15.99)
- Be a Freelance Journalist (£8.99)
- Be a Freelance Secretary (£8.99)
- Be a Local Councillor (£8.99)
- Be an Effective School Governor (£9.99)
- Become a Freelance Sales Agent (£9.99)
- Become an Au Pair (£8.99)
- Buy & Run a Shop (£8.99)
- Buy & Run a Small Hotel (£8.99)
- Cash from your Computer (£9.99)
- Career Planning for Women (£8.99)
- Choosing a Nursing Home (£8.99)
- Claim State Benefits (£9.99)
- Communicate at Work (£7.99)
- Conduct Staff Appraisals (£7.99)
- Conducting Effective Interviews (£8.99)
- Copyright & Law for Writers (£8.99)
- Counsel People at Work (£7.99)
- Creating a Twist in the Tale (£8.99)
- Creative Writing (£9.99)
- Critical Thinking for Students (£8.99)
- Do Voluntary Work Abroad (£8.99)
- Do Your Own Advertising (£8.99)
- Do Your Own PR (£8.99)
- Doing Business Abroad (£9.99)
- Emigrate (£9.99)
- Employ & Manage Staff (£8.99)
- Find Temporary Work Abroad (£8.99)
- Finding a Job in Canada (£9.99)
- Finding a Job in Computers (£8.99)
- Finding a Job in New Zealand (£9.99)
- Finding a Job with a Future (£8.99)
- Finding Work Overseas (£9.99)
- Freelance DJ-ing (£8.99)
- Get a Job Abroad (£10.99)
- Get a Job in America (£9.99)
- Get a Job in Australia (£9.99)
- Get a Job in Europe (£9.99)
- Get a Job in France (£9.99)
- Get a Job in Germany (£9.99)
- Get a Job in Hotels and Catering (£8.99)
- Get a Job in Travel & Tourism (£8.99)
- Get into Films & TV (£8.99)
- Get into Radio (£8.99)
- Get That Job (£6.99)
- Getting your First Job (£8.99)
- Going to University (£8.99)
- Helping your Child to Read (£8.99)
- Investing in People (£8.99)
- Invest in Stocks & Shares (£8.99)

- Keep Business Accounts (£7.99)
- Know Your Rights at Work (£8.99)
- Know Your Rights: Teachers (£6.99)
- Live & Work in America (£9.99)
- Live & Work in Australia (£12.99)
- Live & Work in Germany (£9.99)
- Live & Work in Greece (£9.99)
- Live & Work in Italy (£8.99)
- Live & Work in New Zealand (£9.99)
- Live & Work in Portugal (£9.99)
- Live & Work in Spain (£7.99)
- Live & Work in the Gulf (£9.99)
- Living & Working in Britain (£8.99)
- Living & Working in China (£9.99)
- Living & Working in Hong Kong (£10.99)
- Living & Working in Israel (£10.99)
- Living & Working in Japan (£8.99)
- Living & Working in Saudi Arabia (£12.99)
- Living & Working in the Netherlands (£9.99)
- Lose Weight & Keep Fit (£6.99)
- Make a Wedding Speech (£7.99)
- Making a Complaint (£8.99)
- Manage a Sales Team (£8.99)
- Manage an Office (£8.99)
- Manage Computers at Work (£8.99)
- Manage People at Work (£8.99)
- Manage Your Career (£8.99)
- Managing Budgets & Cash Flows (£9.99)
- Managing Meetings (£8.99)
- Managing Your Personal Finances (£8.99)
- Market Yourself (£8.99)
- Master Book-Keeping (£8.99)
- Mastering Business English (£8.99)
- Master GCSE Accounts (£8.99)
- Master Languages (£8.99)
- Master Public Speaking (£8.99)
- Obtaining Visas & Work Permits (£9.99)
- Organising Effective Training (£9.99)
- Pass Exams Without Anxiety (£7.99)
- Pass That Interview (£6.99)
- Plan a Wedding (£7.99)
- Prepare a Business Plan (£8.99)
- Publish a Book (£9.99)
- Publish a Newsletter (£9.99)
- Raise Funds & Sponsorship (£7.99)
- Rent & Buy Property in France (£9.99)
- Rent & Buy Property in Italy (£9.99)
- Retire Abroad (£8.99)
- Return to Work (£7.99)
- Run a Local Campaign (£6.99)
- Run a Voluntary Group (£8.99)
- Sell Your Business (£9.99)

How To Books

- Selling into Japan (£14.99)
- Setting up Home in Florida (£9.99)
- Spend a Year Abroad (£8.99)
- Start a Business from Home (£7.99)
- Start a New Career (£6.99)
- Starting to Manage (£8.99)
- Starting to Write (£8.99)
- Start Word Processing (£8.99)
- Start Your Own Business (£8.99)
- Study Abroad (£8.99)
- Study & Learn (£7.99)
- Study & Live in Britain (£7.99)
- Studying at University (£8.99)
- Studying for a Degree (£8.99)
- Successful Grandparenting (£8.99)
- Successful Mail Order Marketing (£9.99)
- Successful Single Parenting (£8.99)
- Survive at College (£4.99)
- Survive Divorce (£8.99)
- Surviving Redundancy (£8.99)
- Take Care of Your Heart (£5.99)
- Taking in Students (£8.99)
- Taking on Staff (£8.99)
- Taking Your A-Levels (£8.99)
- Teach Abroad (£8.99)
- Teach Adults (£8.99)
- Teaching Someone to Drive (£8.99)
- Travel Round the World (£8.99)
- Use a Library (£6.99)

- Use the Internet (£9.99)
- Winning Consumer Competitions (£8.99)
- Winning Presentations (£8.99)
- Work from Home (£8.99)
- Work in an Office (£7.99)
- Work in Retail (£8.99)
- Work with Dogs (£8.99)
- Working Abroad (£14.99)
- Working as a Holiday Rep (£9.99)
- Working in Japan (£10.99)
- Working in Photography (£8.99)
- Working in the Gulf (£10.99)
- Working on Contract Worldwide (£9.99)
- Working on Cruise Ships (£9.99)
- Write a CV that Works (£7.99)
- Write a Press Release (£9.99)
- Write a Report (£8.99)
- Write an Assignment (£8.99)
- Write an Essay (£7.99)
- Write & Sell Computer Software (£9.99)
- Write Business Letters (£8.99)
- Write for Publication (£8.99)
- Write for Television (£8.99)
- Write Your Dissertation (£8.99)
- Writing a Non Fiction Book (£8.99)
- Writing & Selling a Novel (£8.99)
- Writing & Selling Short Stories (£8.99)
- Writing Reviews (£8.99)
- Your Own Business in Europe (£12.99)

To: Plymbridge Distributors Ltd, Plymbridge House, Estover Road, Plymouth PL6 7PZ.
Customer Services Tel: (01752) 202301. Fax: (01752) 202331.

Please send me copies of the titles I have indicated. Please add postage & packing (UK £1, Europe including Eire, £2, World £3 airmail).

☐ I enclose cheque/PO payable to Plymbridge Distributors Ltd for £ _____

☐ Please charge to my ☐ MasterCard, ☐ Visa, ☐ AMEX card.

Account No. ☐☐☐☐☐☐☐☐☐☐☐☐☐☐☐☐

Card Expiry Date ☐☐ 19 ☎ **Credit Card orders may be faxed or phoned.**

Customer Name (CAPITALS) ....

Address ....

.... Postcode ....

Telephone .... Signature ....

Every effort will be made to despatch your copy as soon as possible but to avoid possible disappointment please allow up to 21 days for despatch time (42 days if overseas). Prices and availability are subject to change without notice.

Code BPA